ARCHITECTURAL

The Journal of the Architectural Heritage Society of Scotland

HERITAGE II

~

SCOTTISH ARCHITECTS ABROAD

~

EDINBURGH

University Press

1991

The Architectural Heritage Society of Scotland
43b Manor Place, Edinburgh EH3 7EB
Tel. (031) 225 9724

This publication has been generously sponsored by grants from the Ivory Trust and the British Academy, to whom the Society wishes to express its gratitude.

Manuscripts for submission to *Architectural Heritage* should be sent to John Lowrey, c/o the Architectural Heritage Society of Scotland, 43b Manor Place, Edinburgh, EH3 7EB.

Architectural Heritage II is the eighteenth issue of *The Journal of the Architectural Heritage Society of Scotland* (formerly the *Scottish Georgian Society*). Backnumbers (1, 7–11, 13, 15) are available from the Society. *Architectural Heritage I: William Adam* (1990) is available directly from Edinburgh University Press.

Membership of the Society entitles members to receive both *Architectural Heritage* and the regular *Newsletters* free of charge. The Society exists to promote the protection and study of Scotland's historic architecture. Details of membership can be obtained from the Society's headquarters.

CONTENTS

DEBORAH HOWARD

Editorial: The Export of Scottish Architectural Talent

> The Scots have made a greater Figure Abroad, than any other Nation in Europe; this hath been generally ascribed to the Barrenness of their Country, as not being able to maintain its Inhabitants: But this is a vulgar Error, for it's entirely owing to the Fineness of their Education.[1]

So wrote Macky in 1723, referring to Scotland's landed gentry, whose younger sons, well-educated but landless, were obliged to seek their fortunes overseas—in Sweden, Muscovy, Poland, Germany, France or Italy. 'In Italy', (he claimed the same of Germany) 'you go nowhere but you meet with Scotch Families'.

Half a century later Dr Johnson was less positive. Dismayed by the scale of emigration from the Western Isles on his visit of 1773, he wrote: 'Some method to stop this epidemic desire of wandering, which spreads its contagion from valley to valley, deserves to be sought with great diligence'.[2] By this time the chief destination was the New World, and the appeal of emigration had permeated down through the social classes. Nevertheless, embarkation was an emotive process. The hardships endured by early Scots settlers in the Americas are vividly told in Sophie Drinkall's article on Jamaica in this volume. Old photographs of Scotland's city streets show posters advertising emigrant voyages pasted to tenement gable ends, still offering a glimpse of hope to the poor and unemployed at the turn of this century.

Almost every craft or profession was exported from Scotland in these waves of emigration.[3] The architects who ventured abroad fall into two distinct categories: those who travelled to learn, and those who took their own talents to foreign lands.

Several instances of travel equipping the architect with both confidence and visual erudition are recounted in this anthology. As early as the 16th century, Sir James Hamilton of Finnart's probable travels to the Continent exposed him to first-hand experience of European architecture at the height of the Renaissance. During the Age of the Grand Tour Scotsmen in Rome, such as James Byres and George Richardson, aimed to acquire both education and social advantages, although Richardson found his inferior position as James Adam's draughtsman rather irksome. Both James Smith and James Gibbs turned from the priesthood to architecture after reacting against the oppressiveness of the Scots College in Rome. Sketching abroad continued to be regarded as an asset to the young architect into our own century, and beautiful published sketchbooks helped to disseminate ideas from abroad.

The fortunes of those architects who went abroad to practise rather than to learn varied considerably. Charles Peterson has recently shown how the Scots architect Robert

Smith, born in Lugton, near Dalkeith in 1722, became the pre-eminent architect in colonial America.[4] Others—such as James Souttar, whose visit to Sweden is discussed here, or the Highland architect William Miller Roberston, who built the mosque in Nairobi in 1911–14[5]—stayed away only briefly. The colonial mentality could make an architect remarkably impervious to the experience of travel, as the career of William Kidner in the Far East, told in this volume, makes depressingly clear. The most extraordinary success story must surely be that of William Hastie, who redesigned almost every town in Russia in the early 18th century, as Dmitri Shvidkovsky relates.

The importance of Scottish architects to the history of English architecture is well recognised: one need only think of Colen Campbell, James Gibbs, Robert Adam and William Chambers in the 18th century. But as this volume shows, their influence extended right across the globe. Scotland's architecture has not evolved as a neatly wrapped, impermeable package, but as if loosely bound in a net, through which ideas filtered in both directions.

University of Edinburgh

NOTES

1. J. Macky, *A Journey through Scotland*, London, 1729, pp. vi–ix.
2. S. Johnson, *Journey to the Western Islands of Scotland*, 1775, Penguin edn., Harmondsworth, 1984, p. 102.
3. See, for example, G. Donaldson, *The Scots Overseas*, London, 1966; and R. Cage, *The Scots Abroad: Labour, Capital, Enterprise 1750–1914*, London, 1985.
4. Charles E. Peterson, 'Robert Smith, Philadelphia Builder Architect: from Dalkeith to Princeton', in Richard B. Sher & Jeffrey Smith, *Scotland & America in the Age of the Enlightenment*, Edinburgh, 1990, pp. 275–299.
5. Information kindly provided by Robertson's grandson, Ross Robertson, of Tain, Ross & Cromarty.

Finnart's Platt

Sir James Hamilton of Finnart (c.1500–1540), second cousin to King James V and thereby a distant relative also of King Henry VIII, was a powerful Renaissance figure of early 16th century Scotland. There is unusual evidence of his direct involvement in some major artillery fortifications, and in two of James V's magnificent palaces. Given the strong probability that he spent some years in France as a young man, his activities provide a focus for the examination of French influence in early 16th-century Scottish architecture.

INSOFAR as retrospective comparisons are illuminating, Sir James Hamilton of Finnart's career seems to fuse the activities of a Borgia or *capo di regime* with the interests of a Lord Burlington. It seems at the least probable that Finnart had an architectural interest to the degree of making 'platts'; and that when the master masons may have queried the matter, Finnart was appointed Master of Works *en chef* for the entire country.

The essence of the argument is founded on records that reveal a deeper involvement in construction than that of overlord–living on site and collecting ironwork–and statements by contemporaries of his sudden fall and execution in 1540. Bishop Lesley, for example, opined that Hamilton had no expectation of death because 'he had been so diligent in the King's service specially in reforming the Palaces of Stirling and Linlithgow and making new lodgings thereto'.[1] Although there is scant documentary evidence of Finnart ever having travelled abroad, or having acted as architect in the way we would understand the term today, grounds for such conjecture are legion. Since the Dictionary of National Biography states (without proof) that Hamilton spent his early years at the French Court,[2] it has seemed apposite to take his career as a catalyst for examining French influence upon Scots Renaissance architecture.

Loire and Breton connections, in particular, would repay scrutiny, since Scots seeking to avoid English interception by travelling down the west coast would almost certainly have landed in Brittany, if they were not to go further south to La Rochelle or Bordeaux. Many characteristics of 16th-century Scottish architecture are visible there: new work often extends from, or is attached to, older:–even the most jewel-like Renaissance chateau, Azay-le-Rideau, remaining attached to its *tour féodal* until the 19th century. It was more common than not for Brittany *châteaux* to take the form of a U-plan courtyard, not infrequently closed on the fourth side by a screen wall. The plan of Le Riveau, for example, compares closely with the final plan of Pitsligo: a medieval tower linked to a long wing of residential apartments terminating in a round bedroom tower. In Pitsligo's case (Le Riveau's being demolished) the remaining wings provide the gallery and the household and visitors' apartments.

In both France and Scotland, there developed an aesthetic of harled or plastered walls to offset dressed stone details, superstructures, windows, stringcourses and armorial panels. Even at the miniature level of dormer window details, the sunburst or scallop motif that appears in rich merchants' houses in Rochefort-en-Terre in central Brittany, and in its grandest form at Azay-le-Rideau, is also to be found at Claypotts Castle in Dundee. The great aedicules that appear in the gable wall of Aberdour, and as dormer windows at Cullen, (now known to have been offset against plain harling) can be seen in near-identical form as wall-niches in the *château* of Villesavin.

In the early 16th century Scotland was flooded with foreign craftsmen: not ordinary masons but, with unfailing regularity, *master masons*.[3] The discovery of the same mason's initials on the dressed stone (usually corbelling) of different tower houses or palace blocks in the same neighbourhood reveals the possibility that estate or regional masons were largely responsible for the plan form and predominant construction of those great buildings: but also that there was a fraternity of travelling craft masons, some of whom might well have come from abroad, who added expensive dressed embellishments. When the Earl of Huntly sought to repair and enhance his slighted palace block at Strathbogie in 1594, he had to wait for 7 years for the masons 'for masons were not then to be had',[4] eventually using the services of the Englishman Ralph Rawlinson.[5]

In introducing Finnart to the world of building, one can begin by noting the coincidence of his appointments and ownerships with places known to have undergone major building. In November 1526 (an odd date given the circumstances of the King's near captivity by the Douglases and Finnart's murder of the Earl of Lennox), Sir James Hamilton of Finnart was appointed, with his heirs, Captain and Keeper of the Palace of Linlithgow. As the young king's 'lovit familiar' he might well have brought tales of France to the court to blend with the masques of the King's other youthful friend Sir David Lindsay of the Mount. In May 1527, he was appointed Captain of Dumbarton Castle for nine years.[6] He is also known to have had responsibility eventually for Craignethan, the Palace at Stirling, Blackness Castle and Rothesay. Finally, on 9th September 1539, Finnart was appointed 'Master of Work Principal to our Sovereign Lord of all the works within his realm now building or to be built, and to have 3 or 4 deputies under him who shall answer to him and his direction overall'[7] How did this all come about?

MILITARY FORTIFICATIONS

When James V won free of the Douglases in 1528, he besieged their castle of Tantallon—unsuccessfully after its recent military strengthening and re-fortification with earth

1. Craignethan Castle, Clydesdale, from the air. (RCHAMS)

embankments and a peculiar traverse wall ending in a round artillery tower, which had certain echoes of the Dunbar blockhouse. The alliance between Hamiltons and Douglases could have provided Finnart's advice to the latter in the strengthening of Tantallon before the siege, or, more likely, to the King and his master mason George Sempill in the works afterwards, when the rooms in the curtain wall were filled in. It is improbable to suggest that Finnart erupts upon the scene of advanced military fortifications with Craignethan about two years later without having previously taken an interest, and much was clearly under way. With some uncertainty as to date, Pitscottie records James V sending:

> . . . to Flanders, and brought home artillery and harness, with powder and bullets, with picks and all other kinds of munition, and garnished his castles therewith, viz: Edinburgh, Stirling, Dunbar, Dumbarton and Blackness.[8]

No date is known for the construction of the castle of Craignethan in the Clyde Valley, (Fig. 1, perhaps better known as Tillietudlem after it was erroneously identified with the fortress of Scott's *Old Mortality*), save that it emerged between 1530 and 1540. It is well excavated, and can be interpreted with accuracy; but it now appears that Cadzow Castle, the historic seat of the Hamiltons on the banks of the Avon further up the Clyde Valley, which is not well excavated, is in essentials so similar as to postulate the same hand.[9] Craignethan consists of a high, river-girt promontory severed from the hinterland by a deep rock-cut ditch guarded by caponiers. The plateau behind the ditch was almost entirely occupied by a rectangular fortification consisting of an outer curtain wall with square flanking towers and corners, protected from landward attack by a high, thick artillery wall with, it is presumed, gun emplacements along the parapet.

The strangely symmetrical plan appears to have few prototypes unless one goes back to Edward I's castles. On the other hand, the fortification of a rock-cut promontory with encircling walls and towers enfolding a greater tower, although rare in Britain, is not unusual in Europe—for example at Chinon, or perhaps—on a much grander scale—the fortifications in Roussillon. The central tower at Craignethan is curious in that the surviving storeys, which would have been harled up to the dressed stone parapet, are almost entirely devoid of any form of embellishment or decoration: and indeed, graced with very few windows. The plan of this tower is unique: apparently an enormous ground-floor hall, with its own private rooms attached with a private staircase going upstairs to undetermined chambers above. There are also two other staircases. If the principal apartment was indeed on the ground floor, in a relatively unwindowed room in a relatively un-decorated block, one can only conclude that Craignethan was a bolt-hole or place of last resort: a *Führerbunker* rather than a living unit—despite its big pleasure garden.

Insofar as it can be ascertained that Cadzow was comparable, and may also display the hand of Finnart, one must conclude that Cadzow cannot be identified with the original Hamilton Palace as has been conjectured. One of the greatest families in the land, the Hamiltons were second in blood to the royal succession. In keeping with the normal practice of the 16th century, their establishment would have been enormous, comprising substantial numbers of people fixed to a semi-formal processional sequence of rooms: indeed, rooms that were to be furnished with King James V's furniture which the 2nd Earl of Arran purloined once he gave up the Regency in 1554. The narrow fortification at Cadzow (Fig. 2), beautifully situated on the edge of the High Parks of Hamilton on a cliff above the Avon opposite Chatelherault, simply does not fit. Both it and Craignethan were off the mainstream, remote—even by the standards of the time—and not large. Neither—even at the peak of their defensiveness—would have defeated a determined enemy army, as had Tantallon.[10]

As Captain of Linlithgow, Finnart assumed responsibilities for the castle of Blackness, which protected Linlithgow's port and also enfolded an older tower (a state prison) at its centre. A castle on a promontory, its shape was determined by the ship-shape of the promontory which was separated from the mainland by a rock-cut ditch. Finnart so

2. Fragmentary remains of unexcavated Cadzow Castle on a cliff above the Avon. (RCAHMS)

fortified that wall facing the mainland with heavy masonry and gun emplacements that it is clear that he was relying – as in Cadzow and Craignethan – upon sheer mass and reasonable artillery for defence.

CHURCHES

There is an odd coincidence in new works to the town's churches in Stirling and Linlithgow at the time when major building works are being undertaken in the respective palaces. In both cases, the work is by the town's mason, but certain similarities hint a common influence. In 1529 the Town's Mason of Stirling began a new apse to the choir in the Holy Rude Parish Church: and in 1531, the Town's Mason of Linlithgow was likewise employed. The window tracery, buttresses, and the niches in those buttresses of the two great churches are alike, and in both, the apses are of the highest quality masonry. In architectonic terms, they appear tacked on to their churches, protruding almost in the manner in which some of the chapels in the French *châteaux* protrude. As though to underscore the possible connection with palace rebuilding, one of the corbels in the Holy Rude Church sits upon a column of twisted rope or barley sugar: a cheeky echo, perhaps, of what was being applied to the facade of the Palace uphill.

PALACES AND LODGINGS

The prototype for the new Scots Renaissance palace was probably the vanished Holyrood of James IV, and one wonders if it was at all reflected in the timber palace built by the Earl of Atholl in July 1531 for the progress of James V, his Court and his ambassadors, whose lavishness stunned the Ambassador of the Pope who had adverted to the nickname given to Scotland by other countries—'the arse of the world'. The description of this 'curious palace' is given by Pitscottie:

> Which was builded in the midst of a fair meadow, a fair palace of green timber, wind and green birkes, that were green both under and above, which was fashioned in four quarters, and in every quarter and nuik thereof a great round, as it had been a block-house, which was lofted and gested the space of a three house height; the floors laid with green scarets and spreats, medwarts and flowers, that no man knew whereon he zeid but as he had been in a garden. Further, there were two great rounds in ilk side of the gate, and a great portcullis of tree, falling down with the manner of a barrace, with a drawbridge, and a great stank of water 16 foot deep, and 30 foot abreadth. And also this palace within was hung with fine tapestries and arrasses of silk and lighted with fine glass windows in all airths . . .'[11]

The expense of this affair cost the Earl of Atholl £1,000 per day. To put that into perspective, in three days, the expense approached the cost of building an entire wing in Linlithgow or Stirling Palaces.[12]

The specific plan form Pitscottie mentions is of the greatest interest: being virtually identical to the Château de Bury, on the Loire, the Palace of Boyne near Portsoy whose construction was to begin within about 20 years, and a variation on the original full plan for Holyrood. Even today, it may be seen, for example, in Plessis-Bourrée, not far from Angers.

On 1st February 1535, Sir James Hamilton of Finnart assumed responsibility for the building and repair the Palace of Linlithgow (Fig. 3), and, shouldering aside Sir Thomas Johnston to act in the capacity of its Master of Works, sponsored Thomas French (who was already on site) as King's Master Mason for life. Until 1540, Finnart was responsible for expending sufficient money, £4,500 at the very least, to rebuild an entire wing of the Palace.[13] But that is not what he did.

Finnart's activity appears to have been concentrated in the south and west wings, both of which were already substantially complete. From February 1534, 80-odd cartloads of stone trundled each week up to the palace walls for about a year, to supply Thomas French and his 10 masons and 4 barrowmen with materials. The King expressed his delight the result by awarding France (sic) a £20 bounty on 12th April 1535: 'He has done us for his part great pleasure'. It was equivalent to half his annual salary. The accounts reveal timberwork and lead for the roofs, a great deal of timber including floorboards and wainscotting, substantial ironwork, 'window furnishing', padlocks,

3. The Palace of Linlithgow from the air. Finnart may have been responsible for the forework, the causeway, and much work within the two wings nearest to the camera. (RCAHMS)

ironwork in the chapel; painting the chapel walls, glasswork for the 5 chapel windows with painted glasswork, and painting external sculpture work–the Lion and the Unicorn that stood upon the fore entry.[14]

This was the time that the new entry from the south replaced the outmoded east entry; the outer forework, and the new causeway between the two and around the south of the palace, were built; and the major rooms–particularly the Lion Chamber, the Chapel, and the King's own chambers–refitted. It seems arguable that Finnart was also responsible for the fountain, and some of the great carvings that decorate the inner walls. In modern parlance, this sounds like a high-quality fashionable retro fit. The costs were virtually equal to the construction of a new wing *de novo*. He was not titular Master of the Works–that being the role of Sir Thomas Johnston. He was the 'onlie begetter'– organiser, controller of a large body of skilled and unskilled men, purchaser of materials: no figurehead.

Finnart's appointment as Master of Work Principal in 1539 brought him the munifi- cent salary of £200 per annum, five times that of Master Mason Thomas French. On 1st

January 1540, all captains, constables and keepers of Royal castles, houses, palaces and fortalices were required to give Sir James Hamilton of Finnart and his servants access as often and as necessary to let them modify, mend and build 'where myster [necessity] is'.[15] That appointment is for no mere financial controller, and it was the summit of his non-political career.

So what was Hamilton's role in the 'pretty palace in the castle of Stirling' (as Pitscottie called it)? At his lodgings, Mrs Atkins fed him and his suite lavishly 'the time he remained there upon the building of the new work', and the consensus is that he had the administrative and financial responsibility for the new palace, and probably provided a 'platt' or plan (perhaps in the manner of Henry VIII).

The designer of the 'new work' of Stirling began with a difficult, uneven, and almost rhomboid site constrained to the east by the great curtain wall and Prince's Tower of James IV's work, to the north by the corner of his Great Hall, to the west by the now demolished chapel and the King's Old Buildings, and to the south by a cliff out over which the now missing west wing was corbelled or cantilevered. The site also slopes steeply to the north, and was occupied by substantial existing buildings which the RCAHMS believe were incorporated to an undetermined degree.[16] At the very least, they provided the new palace with its platform and perhaps some of the walls. It is scarcely credible that this enormous mass of building, with its high craft exterior could have been completed from scratch within two years. The Palace of Stirling, that is to say the palace *block* at Stirling (in contradistinction to Linlithgow, Falkland and Holyrood which were palaces *tout entier*), is an amazing extravagance: a single-storied quadrangle (Fig. 4) supported on under building to the north, with—so it appears— virtually no ancillary or supporting apartments to service the two ceremonial suites of King's and Queen's Royal apartments. There is no evidence what rooms were contained within the missing west wing, nor in the upper storey. Where were the rooms for the Officers of State, the Baronage, poets, chancellors and chamberlains—those who were accommodated in the second great courtyard at Holyrood? Even if some were on the upper floor of the palace block, their windows looking solely into the courtyard, there is no trace of a staircase sufficiently grand for this purpose.

Deprived of their intended wall-painting, wainscotting (for there was such at Linlithgow), arras, tapestries and timber panelled ceilings, all that remains in the cavernous royal suites are the immense window embrasures and the huge fireplaces. With the exception of the delicately pilastered and panelled fireplace in the King's bedchamber, these fireplaces appear enormous and gross—even assuming that the sculptures would have been gilt—principally because the lintels, columns and feet (as will be seen) were never completed with their intended countersunk carvings.

The plan is unique. The building is less a palace than a Royal Pavilion—a compact jewel around a tight courtyard, in which the suites of three processional rooms—instead of

4. The west facade of the Royal Pavilion in the Castle of Stirling. Note how the parapet does not exactly line up with the boys. (RCAHMS)

being above each other (Holyrood), or separated around a much wider quadrangle (Linlithgow), are designed in compact so that the King and Queen's bedrooms abut.

The facade, however, reeks of compromise with existing structures. The regularity of Falkland was impossible in Stirling where the tight improbabilities of the site were camouflaged by a beautiful skin of smooth ashlar—possibly the best in all James V's building works. At Stirling the design is composed of projected and recessed bays, like enormous pilasters with niches between.

The exterior has been attributed to influence from the Loire *châteaux*.[17] A study of Loire *châteaux*, most built during the reign of François 1er however, gives little support to this thesis. Although the facade is indeed French in derivation, it has more affinity to the 'style Louis XII' (1495–1515); a style in turn much influenced by the Lombardic following the establishment in 1495 of the Colony of Amboise with Italian craftsmen, notably Fra Giovanni Giocondo. In Stirling, the characteristics of this style have been seized and transformed from decoration into a complete architecture. Essential elements have been characterised thus:

> Openings were deeply recessed, often fringed with an order of hanging cusping and sheltered under a hood mould, sometimes of ogee form, carried on corbels set below the springing . . . In arches and openings, the prevailing pointed form was replaced with growing frequency by the circular and eliptical or quasi-eliptical with 3 or 5 centres or by flat lintels . . .[18]

Other characteristics of this style apposite to Stirling were sunken carved faces, piers square set anglewise, or circular with spiral decoration, and facades peopled with figures with supple bodies and writhing limbs. The square cusped niche in the Louis XII wing at Blois appears at Linlithgow, and the *château* of Brézé displays a semi-circular cusped arch above a doorway. Most distinctive, however, are the entrance to the Ducal Palace at Nancy, home of the Guise Cardinal of Lorraine, the great staircase at Châteaudun and the Breton *château* of Josselin, remodelled in the late 1490s. One of the Josselin's tall dormer windows is enclosed within a flamboyant cusp, and the bays of its residential wings are punctuated by tall rope-work columns. John Dunbar has pointed out that the alternation of windows and niches (albeit otherwise wholly different) appears in the 1531 Hôtel de Ville of Paris,[19] and Stirling's arrangement of sculpture recalls that of the Château d'Usson. It is not at all improbable that Finnart absorbed such influences if he did indeed visit France as a young man. He was given little opportunity to do much to the facade of Linlithgow, but, given the opportunity of a smallish, purpose-designed royal pavilion at Stirling, he could have produced a synthesis from which the master masons could work. The Louis XII style attribution would also go a long way to explain the crude barrenness of the palace chimneypieces. They were almost certainly due for rich countersunk carving in the manner of the King's bedroom, but were left, like the interior as a whole, unfinished.

The notion of Finnart acting *qua* Burlington in providing a 'platt' is supported by examining the inconsistencies in the facade (Fig. 4). Nothing quite lines up, and the impression of symmetry is illusory. The statue of King James in the north-west corner does not exactly match that of (presumably) the Queen which is not exactly on the north-east corner, but round the side; the crenellations of the parapet appear to match the windows, but can be seen on the west flank to be out of step. Things are not quite right; implying not just the retention of some obdurate earlier building to make things difficult, but a failure by a pragmatic master mason to appreciate and achieve the precision of a symmetrical design imposed by another.

During the building of Stirling, Finnart lived on site, and his personal involvement is implied by his collecting window ironwork from Linlithgow. Using the multiplier of 1000, that bill for Finnart's victuals from Mrs Atkins amounted to £65,000: and there is no evidence that it was the only bill or that it covered lodgings. It implies a long stay, large household and lavish entertainment.[20]

The Louis XII architecture of the exterior of the Palace of Stirling is remarkably old-fashioned when compared to its exact contemporaries Falkland Palace and Holyrood. They are a generation apart: if Stirling and Linlithgow were inspired by a *style Louis XII* that of Falkland is certainly François 1er.[21] The origins of the magnificent, glittering, almost Tudor frontage of Holyrood (Fig. 5)—the queen of the Royal palaces and the Escorial of Scotland—still defy research. Falkland and Holyrood were the direct responsibility of the 'Supreme Master of Works' John Scrymgeour, whose architectural taste

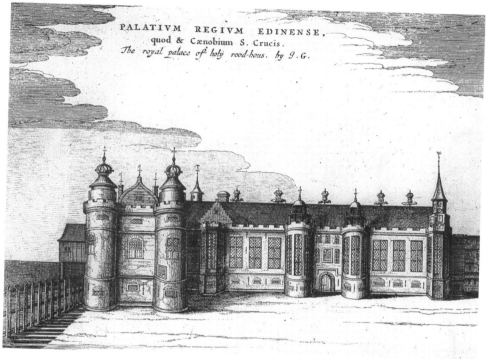

5. Holyrood Palace drawn by James Gordon of Rothiemay in 1647. (RCAHMS)

indicates a more contemporary awareness of trends in France than Finnart. He is clearly a man about whom much might be learnt.

The King's rate of expenditure was lavish: he spent something over £15,000 at Falkland,[22] which approximated to some £5,000 per wing, for Falkland was only three-sided; and much of that was the refacing of an existing building (Fig. 6). Between 1534–9, he spent at least £4,500 in Linlithgow, and untold sums at Holyrood. An indication of the gorgeousness that the King planned in the west of Scotland is the grant to Finnart of approximately £2,100 in April 1540 to reform the Palace of Rothesay.

Stirling's finances are opaque. Based on the cost of Falkland, a completely new four-sided courtyard at the palace of Stirling could well have been expected to cost approximately £16,000. No such figures appear in the accounts. On 9th October 1539, Finnart is paid £4,000 'to complete' the King's work at Stirling, followed by a quitclaim for a further £4,000 the following month 'for payment of the said sum, the said James has given his obligation to our Sovereign Lord to complete his work which he has begun'.[23] £8,000 would only have been sufficient had Finnart been finishing off a substantial pre-existing building. Coincidentally, the period of the work upon Stirling is the one during which the King makes such lavish gifts of land to Finnart; and these

6. Falkland Palace courtyard by John Slezer c.1680. (RCAHMS) Looking back over Figures 3–6 one cannot fail to be impressed by the scale and magnificence of James V's building operations.

lead to the supposition that Finnart was undertaking much of the work at his own expense, being recompensed by gifts of territory, post-hoc facto. It was how Finnart came to hold Evandale, granted by the King on 22nd September 1539 in recognition of his 'service in the completion at great cost of the Palaces of Linlithgow and of Stirling'.[24] Much of the money for this building came from the church, who had offered James V lavish bribes to 'abjure Martin Luther'; possibly in recognition of which, Finnart was appointed as his fervent justiciar to join the clerics in the increasingly frequent trials of heretics.

Perhaps by 1540, the money was running out; mayhap Finnart was pressing for a further instalment; perhaps he had even used some of his half-brother's family patrimony to fund the King's works. Whatever which way, in mid flood of his architectural appointment, just as he was about to begin on Rothesay, fit out the interior of Stirling, and complete Linlithgow, Sir James Hamilton of Finnart's many enemies achieved his removal. He was arrested on 16th July, accused of treason by way of an assassination attempt some years earlier, and the shooting of Linlithgow cannon at the King earlier that year. He was dead–protesting his innocence in terms very similar to Cardinal Wolsey–on the 16th August.

Forfeiture of his immense properties would replenish the Royal coffers, and one beneficiary was his half-brother, the Earl of Arran,[25] who probably had a hand in the conspiracy. It was a truly Renaissance fate. As the 16th-century Scots proverb has it: *A swine that is fat is the cause of his own death.*

Royal Incorporation of Architects in Scotland

ACKNOWLEDGEMENTS

This paper owes an immense debt to Iain MacIvor and John Dunbar for their researches and assistance. Valuable help was also proffered by Dr David Walker, Prof Gordon Donaldson, Donald Galbraith, Denys Pringle, Dr Ronald Cant, Anne O'Connor and Aonghus McKechnie. None is committed to agreeing.

NOTES

1. John Lesley, Bishop of Ross, *The History of Scotland . . . to the year 1561*, Bannatyne Club, Edinburgh, 1830.

Finnart's broader career of bloodshed and politics, the 'Bastard-smaik' (illegitimate scoundrel) in the words of his uncle Sir Patrick Hamilton, is outlined in more detail in a fuller version of this article in the RIAS Library.

2. *Dictionary of National Biography*, p. 1050.

3. Walter Merlioune (of Edinburgh's Marlin's Wynd) was master-mason working at Stirling and responsible for a now missing tower at Holyrood, and is thought to have paved the causeway of the High Street. Thomas French (or France) was master-mason at Linlithgow, earning James V's undying gratitude, and Moyse Martin, appointed Master Mason to the Crown in 1536, worked on the blockhouse at Dunbar and possibly on Blackness. Nicholas Roy was appointed master-mason at Falkland in April 1539. Andrew Mansioune was possibly the carver of the Stirling Heads, and Peter Flemishman carved the statues on the facade of Falkland Chapel.

(John Dunbar, *French Influence in Scottish Architecture during the 16th century*, The Scottish Records Association Conference Report, 1989).

4. *Calendar of State Papers*, 1595.

5. *Works Accounts 11*, p. 213 (ex. info John Dunbar).

6. Robert Pitcairn, *Criminal Trials in Scotland*, Vol 1, Edinburgh 1833, (and notes from Appendix stated as being from the Register of Privy Seal), p. 241.

7. Iain MacIvor, *Hamilton of Finnart*, Unpublished paper, 1991.

8. Robert Lindsay of Pitscottie, *The History of Scotland from 1436 to 1565*, 3rd Edn., Edinburgh, 1778, p. 229.

Iain MacIvor has speculated that the bumps in the unexcavated moat at Tantallon might yet transpire to be caponiers of the type discovered at Finnart's own stronghold of Craignethan.

9. Denys Pringle discussion of Cadzow excavations.

10. It is perhaps worth remembering that the 2nd Earl of Arran was well known to be propense to wavering: a weak, vacillating man, who had

inherited a position of enormous power, without the strength of character to wield it. One of the many reasons underlying the conspiracy to remove Sir James Hamilton of Finnart could be that he was seen as being the force behind the Hamiltons, and that by his removal, the family could be neutralised. Equally, the weak Earl may well have resented his bastard brother's power, and envied him his lands. It may not be a coincidence that a significant beneficiary from Finnart's forfeiture was the Earl of Arran.

See: Pitcairn; *op. cit.*, p. 255.
11. Pitscottie, *op. cit.*, p. 277.
12. In modern parlance, it seems unlikely that it would have been less than £3 million. Comparative costs are difficult since items decrease or increase in relative cost according to technology. The Scottish pound might best be compared to a French franc. Yet a multiplier from Scots pounds then to British pounds now of 1000 seems reasonable. A complete wing of Linlithgow Palace now, even assuming modern technology and materials, would be little short of £4 millions; and a salary of £40,000 for the Master of Works (now main contractor) not immensely distant from reality.
13. Discussions with Iain MacIvor.
14. *Accounts of the Masters of Works*, Vol 1, pp 115–131.
15. Iain MacIvor, *op. cit.*, quoting from the Register of the Privy Seal.
16. RCAHMS *Stirlingshire*, HMSO, London, 1963, Vol 1, p. 200.
17. *Ibid.*
18. W.H. Wand, *The Architecture of the Renaissance in France*, London (n.d.), Vol 1, pp 4–42.
19. John Dunbar, *Letter*, 3.3.91.
20. Pitcairn, *op. cit.*, p. 316.

Iain MacIvor has adumbrated the delightful possibility that our interpretation of the Stirling Royal Pavilion is misconceived; that the Duke of Albany's French masons who accompanied him to Scotland in 1515 (in full flood of the Louis XII style) began a high, vertical, several storeyed pavilion in Stirling, but left it unfinished. The absence of accounts could be explained by their being from Albany rather than the infant king, and their returning to France with him in 1523. The consequence would be that Finnart was imported in 1538 to finish off and truncate the building, which he did with roof, carvings and parapet (which did not quite fit).
21. John Dunbar has suggested that Falkland's distinctive design derives from François 1er's own *château* of Villers-Cotterets (Aisne) begun in 1533 (Letter of 14.3.91).
22. John Dunbar, letter 14.3.91.
23. Iain MacIvor, *op. cit.*
24. Iain MacIvor, *op. cit.*
25. Pitcairn, *op. cit.*

BIBLIOGRAPHY

George Buchanan, *The History of Scotland*, revised by Mr Bond; Glasgow, 1799; Anon, *A Diurnal of remarkable Occurrents*, Bannatyne Club, Edinburgh, 1833; Iain MacIvor, *Artillery and Major Places of Strength in the Lothians and the East Border 1513–1542*; Cauldwell (Ed.), *Scottish Weapons and fortifications 1100–1800*, 1981; Iain MacIvor, *Craignethan Castle*, HMSO; RK Hannay (Ed.), *The letters of James V*, Edinburgh, 1954.

James Byres of Tonley (1734–1817): The Architecture of a Scottish Cicerone

A preliminary study of the architectural work of one who has always been better known as an antiquarian, dealer and guide. He is deserving of wider recognition as an architectural draftsman of great sensitivity.

. . . one of those gentlemen who, with a little income, a little knowledge of art, and a full capacity for speech, wanders from gallery to gallery, delivering opinions on the work of genius with a confidence that passes with the world for the offspring of refined taste.[1]

WITH these words Sir Henry Raeburn is supposed to have damned a man to whom at other times he considered he owed what little benefit he gained from his visit to Rome.

James Byres, eldest son of Patrick Byres of Tonley, an Aberdeenshire laird of choleric temper and Jacobitish tendencies, arrived in Rome in 1757 (Fig. 1). His intention was to study architecture and his first success was to win the third prize in the Concorso Clementino of the Accademia di San Luca in 1762 with the design for an enormous baroque palace of staggering complexity and monumentality.[2] It was noticed in the journals,[3] and Betty Adam in a letter to her brother was to write:

We imagine Mr Byres, when he comes home, if he settles in England will cut out Blackfriars Mylne, having taken the prize of a great calling: there is a great puff about it in the newspapers.[4]

Architecture was not to be the field in which Byres was to succeed. Far more profitable were his activities as a guide and mentor to rich Britons who were flocking to Rome, and as a dealer between the collectors and artists who were waiting to supply their needs. He soon established a friendship with Pompeo Batoni, which was to last until the latter's death, and which was to prove a connection of equal benefit to both.[5] Byres had probably been introduced to Batoni by his kinsman, William Mossman, who had studied under Imperiali in the 1730s, and who had commissioned a number of works from Batoni for Captain John Urquhart of Craigston.[6]

Byres' activities as an antiquary and as a guide and dealer have been well researched,[7] and will continue to be as fresh material comes to light. His architectural works have received little attention; most writers are happy to parrot the phrases 'frozen baroque', 'grandiose compositions in the late Roman Baroque tradition of Fuga and Vanvitelli' and 'distinctly retardaire in style'. It would be perverse to claim that he was an architect of any great ability: his large designs have all the eye-catching qualities and practical disadvantages that distinguish the work of too many competition winners, but his work has a certain charm.

1. The Byres Family, by F. Smuglewicz, c. 1779. James Byres is second from the left pointing to a map of Rome. (National Galleries of Scotland)

It is perhaps fortunate that none of his large houses was built. With their uncomfortable attempts to graft Roman elevations onto English Palladian plans they would have been unlikely to have survived. His smaller works, generally those that were executed, are of a very different quality, sculptural in form, delicate in detail and elegant in proportion.

The earliest known work is the signed monument to Sir James MacDonald in Sleat Kirk on Skye (Fig. 2). Boswell recalls that it was made in Rome,[8] and it was probably commissioned in 1765, the year before Sir James's death. It takes the form of an aedicule and employs the Roman Doric order after Vignola. On the same wall is a similar monument, less correct or more freely handled (Fig. 3). Although the inscriptions on it are mid-19th century it is difficult to believe that the monument itself can be the work of an Inverness sculptor unless working to a Byres design.

The year 1768 saw Byres produce designs for two buildings in Edinburgh, and this suggests that he may have been in Scotland the previous year, possibly in connection with

2. Monument to Sir James MacDonald, Sleat Kirk, Skye, 1765–68. (RCAHMS, photo by Ian Stuart)

3. Monument in Sleat Kirk—a companion to the MacDonald Monument. Probably from a design by Byres and used at a later period. (RCAHMS, photo by Ian Stuart)

the MacDonald monument. The first was for an enormous *palazzo* for Sir Lawrence Dundas on the east side of St Andrew's Square in the newly laid out New Town, an introduction he may have owed to Thomas Dundas, who had been in Rome in 1764 and had been painted by Batoni. The house is on the grandest scale, on four floors, separated from the square by a large courtyard surrounded by colonnades, with the upper floors dignified by the only example of an open portico known to have been designed by Byres. The rooms are arranged around a square hall or roofed *cortile* which rises through four floors to an attic. The interiors are richly treated with painting and decorative plaster-work, but are remarkably inconvenient in their arrangements. Sir Lawrence was eventually to employ Sir William Chambers to build his house on this site.

The other Edinburgh project was for a new library for the College of Physicians (Figs. 4 & 5). The proposal to build a new library had been under discussion since 1756, and in 1762 the College had accepted the plan submitted by George Fraser, Depute Director of Excise and 'well skilled in Architecture', but had not carried it forward. Byres

4. Elevation of project by James Byres for Physicians' Library, Edinburgh, 1768. (RCAHMS)

submitted two versions of his design, which was probably intended for the site in George Street. It was a loss to Edinburgh that it was never built. Based on the Pantheon, a pedimented front to the street with a recessed portico gave access to two floors of meeting rooms and offices, beyond which lay the circular, domed library. The building was raised above street level and approached by a broad flight of steps. It is perhaps the finest of all Byres' designs.[9]

1770 saw Byres completing two commissions which he received in Rome. Sir Watkin Williams-Wynn had been in Italy in 1768–69 and had sat for Batoni. He wished to rebuild his seat at Wynnstay in Wales and Byres produced designs for this. The mansion was designed on the largest scale, the central block measuring 175 feet by 130 feet (Fig. 6). As at Dundas House the rooms were planned around an enclosed *cortile*. It would have been the grandest building ever erected in the Principality, but was probably beyond the means even of the Williams-Wynn fortune. In Rome the project was the subject of

5. Section through the scheme for the Physicians' Library, Edinburgh, 1768. (RCAHMS)

considerable interest: Dr Charles Burney, on presenting his letters of introduction to James Byres, found him with 'two great professors who came to see his designs for Sir Watkin Williams-Wynn's house, which is a noble one indeed',[10] and Father John Thorpe, writing to Lord Arundel, describes it as having 'been universally admired by the virtuosi'.[11]

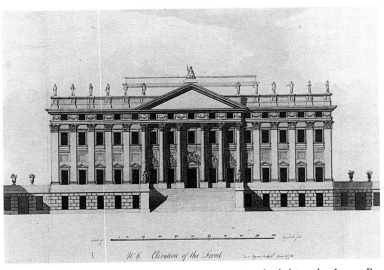

6. Elevation of principal front of project for Wynnstay, Denbighshire, by James Byres, 1770. (National Library of Wales)

The second commission of 1770, which Byres owed to Father Thorpe, was for the altar for the chapel at Wardour Castle, where Lord Arundel was planning a new house. Byres was sent the plans and elevations of the new chapel, and he submitted three designs. These arrived at Wardour in 1772 by the hand of a rich West Indian, but were never used.[12]

Father Thorpe reported that Byres was planning to be in England in 1772. The journey was extended to Scotland, and three commissions—two of them in Aberdeenshire—resulted from it. In the archives of King's College Aberdeen are two sets of drawings relating to proposals to extend the college in 1773. Neither set is signed although a later hand has pencilled in '?Mr Adam'. One scheme intends a mildly Gothic treatment set symmetrically about an old steeple—it is tempting to accept this as his work, for Gothic was not unknown to Byres. The other, in full Roman fig, is almost certainly his. The treatment of the medieval chapel is chaotic: the upper part of the steeple is demolished and the chapel itself is refaced in the Italian manner to match the new building. This is entered by way of a portico taken almost directly from that of the Palazzo Pietro Massimi in Rome, and contains, in addition to some hopelessly unsuitable apartments for the professors and their families, a fine oval library on the first floor. Square pavilions in the manner of the Villa Medici pierce the pantiled roof above the staircases. The entirely Roman effect under an Aberdeenshire sky would have been truly remarkable.

At the same time Byres produced designs for two chimneypieces for a drawing room and a dining room (Fig. 7). The drawings are in the possession of the Royal Bank of Scotland, and this has led to them being assigned to Dundas House. They are in fact for Fyvie Castle, where that for the drawing room is still *in situ* (Fig. 8). Both are recorded in the sale catalogue of 1885 as being 'entirely of white and grey marble', but that in the dining room was removed in the alterations carried out by John Bryce for Sir Alexander Forbes-Leith. The date of 1773 on the drawings suggests that Colonel William Gordon ordered the chimneypieces for the alterations he was then planning to the castle.

On the same visit Byres must have met Sir John Rous, Lord Stradbroke. One says 'must' since three sets of drawings signed by Byres for a large country house are in the Rous papers in the East Suffolk Record Office.[13] Meanwhile he may also have received an order from William Urquhart of Craigston for a chimneypiece. There is a very fine one in the Red Room, in two different marbles and enriched with draped urns. Urquhart was improving the house for his young wife, and there was already a Batoni-Mossman connection.

Byres' visit to England in 1779 seems to have produced no work, but a further visit in 1783 may have led to the alterations to the staircase at Walcot Park, which figure in Lord Clive's accounts for 1786.[14] After this nothing is known of his architectural activities until 1789, when William Bury, 1st Lord Charleville, returned from Rome with the drawings for an enormous house which he intended to build to replace his 17th

7. Design for the drawing room chimneypiece, Fyvie Castle, by James Byres, 1773. (RCAHMS)

century house, Redwood at Tullamore. Again wings and quadrants are attached to an enormous *palazzo*, but the feeling is that Byres was now tired. The long, narrow plan is badly organised: the upstairs corridor is 170 feet long! It was never built.

The Roman years were over: Father Thorpe, writing to Lord Arundel in June 1790, records that 'Mr Byres the Antiquarian has quitted Rome and gone to live in his own country, if he can live in that climate'.[15] He could, and did, for another 27 years. His life was devoted largely to his family, his friends, and improving his estate of Tonley, but he did not forsake architecture completely. Writing in 1797 to Abbé MacPherson, Rector of the Scots College in Rome, about his new college at Aquahorthies, Bishop Hay was able to say that 'Good Mr Byres gave us a plan of the house' (Fig. 9).[16] Planned on three floors with an attic, and with a granite elevation of seven bays, Aquahorthies shows none of the decorative features with which Byres liked to enrich his designs. It relies entirely on its proportions and severity for its effect, and in this it succeeds admirably.

His last work was the handsome mausoleum he designed for his old friend Miss Eliza Fraser at Cluny. This fine domed structure, built in 1807–8 at a cost of £353/19/5 (Fig. 10), should have had a counterpart for his own remains, but for some reason he cancelled his instructions to his trustees.[17] Amongst the Castle Fraser papers are two designs, signed JB, for the sanctuary of a chapel, on square-ended, the other apsidal. Richly decorated with Corinthian columns, the wall behind the altar is furnished with panels

8. Drawing room chimneypiece, Fyvie Castle, 1773. This is the only known executed work by James Byres for which the drawing exists. (RCAHMS)

of the Commandments and the Creed. This could indicate that the building was intended for Episcopalian worship, but its destination is unknown.

Byres' interest in architecture lasted almost to the end: five years before his death he was writing to Hugh Irvine, nephew of his old friend James Irvine who had been a fellow dealer in Rome, on the correct method of designing a mausoleum. He recalls from a distance of nearly 50 years that 'the only Antient Base of the Dorick I ever saw was at Agrigentum it was the Atick base'.[18]

He was to die at his own estate of Tonley at the age of 79 and is now mostly remembered through the letters of his contemporaries as a dealer and guide of a somewhat exhausting nature, and as an early explorer of antiquities. He deserves some little memory as a minor figure in the architectural landscape and as a draftsman of considerable skill.

9. House of Aquahorthie, designed as a Seminary for Bishop Hay by James Byres, 1797. (RCAHMS, photo by Mrs Normile Baxter)

10. Mausoleum of Miss Eliza Fraser, Cluny, designed by James Byres, 1807–8. (RCAHMS, photo by Alastair Rowan)

NOTES

1. Allan Cunningham, *The Lives of the Most Eminent British Painters*, 1879, II, p. 264.

2. The subject of the competition was 'un palazzo in una campagna deliziosa per un gran Principe ed altre Fabbriche separate per altri signori della sua corte, di cui il tutto deve essere circondata da una fossa, e da una strada coperta, per essere di fesa da tutti gli insulti de nemici'. The drawings are in the archives of the Accademia di San Luca, Rome. James Byres was elected Accademico di Merito in 1771. (See M.F. MacDonald, 'Academies of Art', *Leids Kunsthistorisch Jaarboek*, V–VI, 1986–7, pp. 77–94.)

3. *Scots Magazine*, XXIV, p. 611.

4. Robert Milne had acquired a measure of fame as the designer of Blackfriars Bridge.

5. Anthony M. Clark (ed. E.P. Bowron), *Pompeo Batoni*, 1985.

6. Urquhart of Craigston archives, Craigston Castle.

7. David Ridgeway, 'An Eighteenth Century Aberdonian in Italy: James Byres of Tonley and the Etruscans', *Deeside Field*, XIX, 1987, pp. 124–130; idem, 'James Byres and the Ancient State of Italy: Unpublished Documents in Edinburgh', *Atti del Secondo Congresso Internazionale Etrusco (1985)*, 1989; and Harry Gordon Slade, 'James Byres of Tonley 1734–1817: The Aberdeen Years', *Deeside Field*, XIX, 1987, pp. 130–139.

8. James Boswell, *A Journal of a Tour to the Western Hebrides with Samuel Johnson*, Everyman edn., 1948, p. 115, entry for 5 September 1773.

9. Minute books of the College of Physicians, Edinburgh.

10. Dr Charles Burney, *Music, Men and Manners in France and Italy 1770*, ed. H. Edmund Poole, Folio Society, 1969, p. 130.

11. Father Thorpe to Lord Arundel, 12 Dec. 1770.

12. Father Thorpe to Lord Arundel, 26 Oct. 1772.

13. Because of the Rous provenance they are assumed to be for rebuilding Henham Hall for Sir John Rous: they could equally well be for a different building for another client. There is no record for Sir John having made the Grand Tour, so Byres must have picked up this commission in England. As with Wynnstay the central block remains a town *palazzo*, although both versions of the design have service wings connected to the main house by quadrants. See Hugh Honour, 'James Byres' Designs for Rebuilding Henham Hall', *The Country Seat*, ed. H. Colvin and J. Harris, 1970, pp. 164–169. There are no references in the Rous papers to Byres or to these drawings (information from County Archivist).

14. Shropshire Record Office, Powis Papers, 552/9/290.

15. Father Thorpe to Lord Arundel, 16 June 1790.

16. Blairs Paper, BL 4/115/9.

17. H. Gordon Slade, 'Castle Fraser', *Proceedings of the Society of Antiquaries of Scotland*, CIX, 1977–78, pp. 233–300.

18. James Byres to Hugh Irvine, 14 April 1812, Irvine of Drum Archive, Drum.

EXECUTED DESIGNS

SLEAT KIRK, SKYE: Monument to Sir James MacDonald (d. 1766). Probably commissioned 1768. The companion monument in the same kirk may have been made to a design supplied by him.

FYVIE CASTLE, ABERDEENSHIRE: Two chimneypieces for the dining room and drawing room, 1773. That in the dining room was destroyed in 1890. (Drawings held by Royal Bank of Scotland)

WALCOT HALL, SHROPSHIRE: Alterations to the staircase, 1786. This was destroyed in 1933.

HOUSE OF AQUAHORTHIES, ABERDEENSHIRE: 1797. Built as a Roman Catholic Seminary.

CLUNY, ABERDEENSHIRE: Mausoleum for Miss Eliza Fraser of Castle Fraser, 1807. (Specification and contract in Castle Fraser Archive, Mrs Michael Smiley)

CRAIGSTON CASTLE, ABERDEENSHIRE: (Attrib.) Chimneypiece in the Red Room, 1773.

UNEXECUTED DESIGNS

EDINBURGH: House in St Andrew's Square, 1768, for Sir Lawrence Dundas. (RIBA Drawings Collection)

EDINBURGH: Two designs for a Library for the College of Physicians, 1768. (Royal College of Physicians)

WYNNSTAY, DENBIGHSHIRE: Mansion for Sir Watkin Williams-Wynn, 1770. (National Library of Wales)

WARDOUR CASTLE, WILTSHIRE: Three designs for an altar for Lord Arundel, 1770. (Lord Talbot of Malahide)

KING'S COLLEGE ABERDEEN: Design for additions and alterations to King's College, 1773. A second scheme in the Gothick style may also be by Byres. (Aberdeen University Library)

HENHAM HALL, SUFFOLK: Two designs for a mansion for Sir John Rous, 1st Lord Stradbroke, 1774. (East Suffolk Record Office)?

CHARLEVILLE FOREST, TULLAMORE, CO. OFFALY: mansion for William Bury, 1st Lord Charleville, 1789. (Photographs in the Irish Architectural Archives)

CHANCEL FOR A CHAPEL: Two designs signed JB, no date. (Mrs Michael Smiley, Castle Fraser)

'The Fittest Place in Europe for our Profession':
George Richardson in Rome

Surviving letters written by George Richardson from Rome in 1761–2,
when he was acting as draughtsman to James Adam, offer a unique picture
of the life and education of a young man of humble station and of slender
means, but with ambition to become an architect in his own right.

ABOUT the European training of several leading Scottish architects
of the eighteenth century we know a good deal. The education in Rome of Robert and
James Adam, for example, can be charted in such detail, due to the survival of some
hundreds of family letters, that it is almost as if we were with the brothers on their Grand
Tours, able to share their experiences in the acquisition of taste, learning, cosmopolitan
sophistication and an enhanced social position. Such first-rate architects, and equally
several of their elders, contemporaries and successors, were largely young men of
comfortable means who came from well-to-do families—educated, well-established
through profitable business activities, or linked to the landed gentry. Colen Campbell
was a laird's son and was himself an advocate. James Gibbs, son of a merchant and a man
with European connections, was originally intended for the priesthood. James Byres
(though antiquarian pursuits rather than architecture claimed his greatest attention) was
another laird's son. John Baxter benefited by his mason father's connections with
aristocratic patrons and went to Rome as a student of architecture. The Adams were rich
indeed by the standards of their young architectural contemporaries, as was Chambers
with his background of European mercantile wealth which afforded him a long and liberal
education. Robert Mylne, of the dynasty of Scottish master-masons, may have lacked the
wealth of some of his rivals but he was nevertheless determined from an early age to be
not just another mason but an 'architect', and to this end moved in elevated social and
artistic circles in Italy. James Stuart and Charles Cameron were certainly less fortunate
in the matter of inherited wealth or social position, but their natural abilities, drive, and
attraction of the right patronage early allowed them to assume the dignity of professional
architects in their own right.

So much for the young men who went to Rome in order to become 'architects' (as
we understand the term, without qualification), a standing to which their education,
family background or circumstances entitled them to aspire. We know very much less
about the office draughtsmen, clerks and assistants to the celebrated architects who were
their fellow countrymen and for whom they worked when their masters had returned
from a continental education to establish themselves in practice in Britain. We know

almost nothing at all about those lucky few who may have had the opportunity to accompany their masters abroad—if those budding architects were very rich and very grand—on their extended tours and periods of study in Europe. In fact George Richardson,[1] who forms the subject of this article, may be unique in the Georgian period as a Scottish draughtsman abroad in attendance on a greater being. Certainly no records of any similar career are known to me. If others they were—and the case of David Martin,[2] who went out to Rome as assistant to Allan Ramsay in 1755, and who later made a creditable career for himself as a portrait painter in his own right seems the only obvious parallel, albeit in another artistic field—it would surely be of the greatest interest to know what they thought of their experiences. What did Richardson and Martin—in their different ways both examples of the drawing-office or studio assistants whom Robert Adam had labelled somewhat contemptuously the 'Myrmidons of Art'[3]—gain from the Grand Tours they undertook willy-nilly? How did they enjoy these travels; what did they make of the opportunities which were open to them for enlarging their horizons; how much did they absorb of the culture which was offered to them vicariously through the circumstances of employment? Did anything of what their masters went to Rome to gain for themselves rub off on these men of lesser social and intellectual status? And was that first encounter with Antiquity, or the world of the Italian *conversazione*, enough to plant the idea of betterment, of future attainment, by the humbler parties in this game of 'improvement', of a rank akin to that which they saw their masters now enjoying? How many, of any nationality, drawing (like Richardson) in the Roman evenings, aspired to learn all they could, and so become, one day, architects themselves? Richardson's letters, highly unusual and perhaps unique documents which are printed here in full for the first time, provide some answers.

George Richardson, a young Edinburgh draughtsman taken to Rome by James Adam in 1760, rose in the world by way of a career as a decorative designer for the Adam brothers in London to become only a minor architect, certainly, but a leading architectural writer whose most enduring achievement was the production of the *New Vitruvius Britannicus*, the successor volumes to those of Campbell, and of Woolfe and Gandon. Two of his letters from Rome to a Midlothian gentleman who appears to have sponsored his career thus far (and whose continued interest is evidenced by the appearance of his name in subscription lists for Richardson's later published books)[4] survive in the National Library of Scotland (MS. 3812, fols. 1–4). Some years ago I drew attention to the interest and importance of these letters.[5] John Fleming had already quoted some passages from them;[6] and recently Damie Stillman,[7] in making very brief but telling citation of two fragments, has further illustrated my points about the letters as a valuable source of information on the attitudes and aspirations of a humble draughtsman when confronted by the grand catalyst that was the Rome of Antiquity, the Renaissance and the Baroque.

The truly memorable themes to emerge from a reading of Richardson's letters are, first, the sense of how Rome was for him, as for Robert Adam, his 'Holy See of Pleasurable Antiquity'; then his feelings about a possible extension of his travels beyond the limits of a conventional Grand Tour; and lastly his clear-eyed attitude to his employer and his own future prospects. Furthermore, we may detect in his writing some evidence of a talent for expression which was to make publishing on architectural, decorative and iconographic themes his true life's work. The clearest indication of the lasting impression that his Italian experiences of the years in which these letters were written had made upon him is to be sought in the descriptive text of three of his later books. 'To invent with Genius and Combine with Taste is the Business of an Architect', Richardson declared—having confidently assumed the status and dignity of the profession—in the dedication of his *Book of Ceilings* (1776) to Lord Scarsdale, patron at Kedleston. Clearly native Genius, encouraged by the inspiration of Antiquity as encountered at first hand in Italy, was to find its life's partner, Taste, on classic ground. Richardson himself was the archetype of 'the discerning traveller', who had gained immeasurably by his Italian experience, and to whom the author directed the Preface of this work: a man who had observed ancient decoration for himself in the Roman villas and sepulchral chambers, and in the luxurious bathing establishments of the Bay of Naples. His *Treatise on the Five Orders of Architecture* (1787) was illustrated by observations made by the author a quarter of a century before on the 'Magnificent Temples, Baths, Theatres, Amphitheatres, Basilicas, Triumphal Arches, And Other Ancient Buildings' of Rome and Italy, as well as Provence and Istria. And in his *Iconology; or, a Collection of Emblematical Figures*, a two-volume English version published in 1779 of Cesare Ripa's celebrated *Iconologia* of 1593 which supplied (as Stephen Orgel had said)[8] 'the quintessential iconographic text in a splendid neo-classic redaction' and thus provided a visual vocabulary for the professional artist of decorative schemes in the antique taste, we hear echoes of these very letters. Richardson remained true to the sentiments which first moved him in 1761, even to the precise turn of phrase. Thus his caption describing the allegorical representation of the City of Rome is expressed in terms very similar to the encomium delivered in the first letter published below; and his descriptions of the emblematical personifications of Painting, Sculpture and Civil Architecture (Fig. 1) are surely enlivened by memories of personal study at the fountainhead itself.[9]

   A few words by way of commentary on the letters may be useful. Letter 1 opens with a burst of the sycophancy customarily used when addressing a patron. The marvellous glory and grandeur of Rome is extolled. The value of this city of ancient wonders as a training-ground is stressed: there the student might find 'the Rule & Standarts of the Moderns'. The ancient buildings are described. These and the Roman collections constitute a 'Magazine for all that is excellent'. The prospect of travel to Sicily and Greece lies in the future. Richardson's appetite for this extension of the Grand Tour has been whetted by his encounter with antiquity in Rome. He states that James Adam

XXXVI.

Published as the Act Directs Dec.ʳ 1777.

1. Allegorical representations of Painting, Sculpture and Civil Architecture, disciplines for the study of which (together with Music) Rome was, as George Richardson's letters indicate, the centre of the world in the age of the Grand Tour. These personifications of artistic accomplishments come from Richardson's *Iconology* of 1779. (National Library of Scotland)

'intends to do great operations' in Rome; and, for his own part, he recognises that his personal training in the city will set him up in life.

Letter 2 begins with mention of the Levantine expedition, now shelved. Events had conspired to make James Adam abandon his wider plans and instead think of returning to London to establish himself in practice with Robert sooner rather than later. The voyage to Greece and Turkey would have been a 'Grand Tour which wou'd have afforded great entertainment, improv'd Taste, & promis'd considerable advantages'. Thoughts of Richardson's sweetheart alone made him pleased to be coming home. There are hints that his difficulties with James Adam would have been magnified had the eastern trip materialised. There is much on grievances: James Adam should have done him better in clothing and kit after his faithful service. There is an amusing narrative of the row over the quality of Richardson's suits. The real significance of this is the indication that even an architect's draughtsman from Scotland felt that he must keep up appearances in Rome. In Greece and especially in Turkey he might dress more humbly, and with additional advantages in terms of security. Clear-eyed about James Adam, Richardson considers the future in Adam employment. He is beginning to show some independence of thought; he asserts his dignity as a result of his Roman training; yet he recognises his dependence on the Adams, 'well knowing my own incapacity, small fortune, want of Books & little hopes of Interest'. He will play for time, and bargain with his usefulness to his master. He looks to the future. He has been amassing a collection of his own drawings done in his own time, a fact which would annoy James Adam were he to find out: Adam was jealous of his assistants making good. The letter ends on a note of self-confidence and independence, a mood strengthened by critical comments on the standards of the *concorsi* of the Academy of St Luke—the *Balestra* and *Clementino*—and the suggestion that the prizes should not be as much vaunted as they were by British winners. By October 1762 George felt as good as his master.

National Library of Scotland

NOTES

1. On Richardson see the entries in Howard Colvin, *A Biographical Dictionary of British Architects, 1660–1840*, London, 1978; and Eileen Harris, *British Architectural Books and Writers, 1556–1785*, Cambridge, 1990.
2. On Martin see Alastair Smart, *The Life and Art of Allan Ramsay*, London, 1952, p. 100.
3. John Fleming, *Robert Adam and his Circle in Edinburgh and Rome*, London, 1962, p. 151.
4. Of Archibald Shiells nothing is known. He is listed as 'Gentleman' in the 1773–4 edition of Williamson's *Edinburgh Directory*, which is organised by professions.

5. *Scottish Architects at Home and Abroad*, National Library of Scotland, Edinburgh, 1978, pp. 32, 59 (nos. 110, 197).

6. Fleming, *op. cit.*, pp. 288, 377, 378.

7. Damie Stillman, *English Neo-classical Architecture*, 2 vols., London, 1988, vol. i, pp. 28, 52.

8. Introduction to the Garland reprint of Richardson's *Iconology*, 2 vols., New York and London, 1979.

9. *Iconology*, vol. 1, pp. 38–9, 73–4.

Note on transcription. The original spelling has been retained, but punctuation has been supplied to aid the reader.

LETTER I

Rome, 11th July 1761

Dear Sir,

As it is now about Four Months since I did myself the pleasure of writing your last I conceive it may not be incongruous nor any way disgustfull to you that I make another repitition of my long Epistles & especially as I judge it incumbent upon me & as it is an excessive Gratification that I have the Liberty to make fresh remonstrances of my coherence & attachment to such a worthy personage and true Benefactor as you. And notwithstanding your long silence for such a long period yet it is evidently my Duty to acknowledge your Beneficence permanently.

Having no correspondence with you ever since we left Scotland (which I cou'd ardently wish were otherwise) I am incapable to conjecture what might be amusing to you for me to relate as far as my weak abilities will admit. But as we are now in the Ancient City of Rome, once the Mistress of the World & till this day superabounds every other place with respect to its numerous curiositys & infinite Antiquities, I have enough of subject to employ my pen about the Ancient Splendour and glory of the buildings of the Ancient Romans, & which are the highest entertainment to every foreigner & convey the greatest Idea of their Grandeur. Had I enough of capacity to make myself intelligible, I shou'd certainly describe some of these Noble Remains & I guess they might give you more amusement than any other subject that I cou'd pretend to, & which I shall make the Substance of this Sheet, and I know you'll always excuse the incorrectness & indistinct combination of my writing, the Effect of weak Intellectuals.

It would be in vain for me to presume to give any thing of an accurate description of Rome's Antiquitys & too arduous a Task, and I realy believe no pen can convey an adequate Idea of their Superior charm, excellence and Infinity. To consider these ancient Monuments, whether in regard of their Magnificent Beauty or Number is matter of great Astonishment & really raise the Grandeur of the Roman Empire to a more elevated Rank than the most elegant descriptions can advance. And these Stupenduous & lasting Works of the Ancients have something of a particular Charm & Majesty no where to be met with in Modern performances, which gives them such an excellent eclat that they justly become the Rule & Standarts of the Moderns by which they ought to coppy after & attract both the Attention & Admiration of every assiduous & inquisitive Artist, and the fittest Object for the advancing of his improvement. These lasting Monuments are to be seen thro' all the Quarters of the City in great plenty, & it begets the greatest consternation when one makes a reflexion what a Number of these Antiquities are dispers'd to other Countrys & still such a vast quantity in Rome and its Environs. Not only are these Noble Structures throughout the Streets and the Gallerys of the Nobility stor'd with the most Select Collections of Curiosities & Antiquities, but also their Villas (several of which in & contiguous to the City) amply Beautified with a variety of choice Antiquities, and round the Courts, the Elevations & principal Stair Cases of a Number of their Palaces are in a most grand and elegant manner profusely embellish'd by a variety of Statues, Busts, Basreliefs and other Fragments of the Glory of their Ancestors. And yet to this day they are finding buried in the Ruins excellent pieces of workmanship of the Ancients & not only worthy for the execution but also for the value of Materials and rarity of the Subjects.

I must certainly not omit to mention briefly some of these Splendid & Sumptuous Edifices. One is at a stand to which of them to ascribe the greatest praise, either on account of grandeur, beauty or proportion. I may begin with the Pantheon, which excited my greatest Curiosity & to which I found the way same day of our arrival. Its grandeur and Magnificence far surpas'd my Ideas & infinitely excell'd every other piece of Architecture that ever I had beheld. There is grandeur, true proportion and harmony thro' the whole, & there I gaz'd with wonder & admiration first at its lofty & Noble Elevation & then at the excellent Beauty & Magnificence of the inside which is no less most admirably adapted & real Symetry in all its parts. That Structure is certainly one of the finest in the World, & challenges the greatest attention. Its ancient form still remains with little other Alterations than Rob'd of its numerous Monuments. Amongst all the Ancient Temples it is the best preserv'd & was one of the Most considerable ones. Its superior Magnitude and great Solidity has certainly resisted the Injuries of time & defy'd the Violence of Barbarians, for notwithstanding the vast devastations Rome has undergone, the Pantheon's stately Columns and Lofty Dome are still the Admiration of every one & have an unparalled Majesty. The 16 Columns of Egyptian Granite of the Portico, & each of an entire piece, are Matter of Astonishment to think that way such large stones were brought from Thebais in Egypt & erected in Rome by Marcus Agrippa. Round the Circumference of the inside are seven principal Chapels, each of which has two lofty Columns & 2 Pilasters of Antique Yellow & the walls of the inside incrusted with different colours of Marble. There are no Windows for the admission of light as the spacious Lanthorn on the top of the famous Dome well supplies the whole temple with abundance of Light.

I shall not add any more here about the august Temple of the Pantheon which was dedicated to all the gods in general, & some says the convexity of the Dome was a resemblance of Heaven. Nor shall I mention any particulars of the Noble remains of the numerous Temples that are still standing, though not so remarkable as the Pantheon yet have the Beauties & proportions of true Architecture, and their Ruins plainly demonstrate their most excellent work- manship & magnificence.

We may now take a slight view of the Triumphal Arches worthy of observation & conducive of Instruction in our way. Amongst which Constan- tine's Arch & and that of Septimus [sic] Severus have the grandest show & are the most considerable. Each of these consist of three Arches, and tho' Titus's Arch has only one yet comes nothing short of the Beauty & Elegance of the other Two. They are all most superbly adorn'd with Basreliefs representing some of the noble Exploits of those Emperors & a variety of Ornaments. These are lasting Monuments to the honour of the Emperors as well as greatness of the Empire, as are also the Columns of Trajan & Antoninus most sublimely carv'd in Basrelief, the whole height of their shafts most exquisite & noble workmanship erected to perpetuate their heroick Actions to posterity.

Several of the principal Piazza's are adorn'd with Egyptian Obelisks carv'd full of Hieroglyphicks & are a particular Embellishment to the City. There cannot be a clearer instance of the Splendor & Magnificence of the Ancient Romans than their Stupendous & Noble Bagnio's, the most remarkable amongst which were those of the Emperors Dioclesian & Antoninus Caracalla. Their remains are evident proofs of their superior Magnitude & Grandeur, & are as surprizing and entertaining sights to a Foreigner as any in Rome. Nor shou'd Titus's Baths be unnoticed for they, like the rest, took up an extensive space & was a glorious Fabrick. They are now allmost in utter Ruins.

Without doubt the Aqueducts were some of the noblest Designs of the Romans, & one of the clearest evidences of their Grandeur. Many remains of them are still standing & convey an exalted Idea of those glorious perfor- mances. There can nothing in the World be more magnificent than Flavius's Amphitheatre. Amongst all the rest it was superior in vastity & extent and still to this day has a most extraordinary Grand Appearance, tho' it has suffer'd greatly by the outrage of Barbarians, and by the injuries of such a long space & also underwent sad devastations under some of the Roman Pontiffs. No less than three different Palaces have been built of its Detrusion & yet this stupendous Pile has a most noble & formidable Aspect. Round its extensive Elliptical Circumference are rang'd in a beautifull symetry four Orders one above another which have a glorious effect, the Inside no less nobly and commodiously adapted for the convenience of the spectators of which it contain'd a prodigious Number. In short this famous Construction affords a most elated Idea of the Roman pomp & Grandeur, and a worthy object of particular observation. The ruins of Marcellus's Theatre has a particular charm & something about it of an extraordinary Beauty. An admirable Harmony & true proportion runs thro' the whole. Nothing can be seen more beautifull, the semicircular Front dress'd with the Dorick & Ionick Orders of a most elegant Structure.

I shall have done saying any more of these sumptuous & most excellent Edifices of the Ancients, to see which going to destruction one is very apt to regret & to wish that they were as lasting as Dignified. Nor shall I enter upon any thing about the Modern Buildings, Churches & Palaces, nor mention any thing particular of the Pompous & religious Functions perform'd here with His holiness at the head, who makes a very sanctified look & his Guards a martial Appearance.

Several of the Nobles have such Valuable Collections of Antiquities in their Gallerys that they are to be seen by Strangers. Several of the most remarkable I hope I shall have the fortune to see before our departure hence which undubitably is at a considerable distance yet (tho' our excursion to Naples & to Sicily is talk'd of to be in a few Months), and as Mr Adam intends to do such great operations in this City it pleases me much that our residence will be so long fix'd in such a proper place for the improvement of our Studys, as it is undoubtedly the fittest place in Europe for our profession. Rome may be said to be a Magazine for all that is excellent in Painting, Sculpture & Architecture. And our practice here will make us more expert for performing our Operations in Greece with Spirit, when our Abode will be in a more fluctuating & unsettled Condition. You cannot imagine how I am elated at the thoughts of our going to these ancient places of Glory & to examine the Works of so many past Ages & celebrated performances of ancient Hero's, and every day think more and more of our Noble Journey, and I am as anxious and hopefull of Improvement as desirous of returning home. The promising Advantages from the first animates me to bear with patience the inconveniences of the latter, which are fewer than I expected & diminish every hour on account of the many amusing and edifying objects & rare opportunitys we're entertain'd with.

My best Compliments to all your Young Family, and I always remain with the most profound Veneration & Esteem, Dear Sir, Your most obedt, and most humble Servant.

G. RICHARDSON

I imagine the inclos'd lines to Henny will pass under same postage, which you'll please to deliver.

Address: To Archbald Shiells Esq
        at his house
        Inverask near Edinbourg
        Inghilterra

LETTER 2

Rome, 10th October 1762

Dear Sir,

The last time I did myself the favour of writing You I mention'd the approaching view that we then had of our Voyage to the Levant. But now that scheme is altogether laid aside for the following reasons. Mr Adam freighted a Danish ship from London to carry us on this voyage from port to port, and when she was proceeding forwards to Leghorn from whence she was to come directly to Civita Vecchia for to take us aboard, was unluckily taken by the Spaniards near about the Gutt of Gibraltar & carried into Algezieras, where I believe she is still detain'd, and it is doubted whether all the Goods aboard will be condemn'd as a lawfull prize, if they can't prove them to belong to a neutral proprietor as well as the Ship. This detention first made a stop of Mr Adams Motions and was a great obstacle to his setting out for the East, being not only disappointed of the Ship, but also depriv'd of all the Effects & Utensils on Board necessary for the Voyage. Upon the back of this retardment we heard the plague was raging all over Turkey, and by a letter that Mr Adam had from his brother of London, was advis'd to give over all thoughts of his intended Voyage, so many cross accidents having fallen in the way & made him lose so much time. And the day following, being 18th Septmr., he told me that he had by that Letter & other circumstances laid aside all thoughts of seeing Greece &ca., & that instead of going to Turkey he was now thinking of returning to England, which piece of news was altogether acceptable to me on Henny's account, but disagreeable on every other, for if we had compleated such a Grand Tour it must certainly have afforded great entertainment, improv'd Taste, & promis'd considerable advantages. But on the other hand by our not going we will undoubtedly avoid many inconveniencys that we wou'd have had to encounter with, incident to long voyages. And it will likewise in great part remove my complaints & difficultys that I started to you in my last Letter, which long harangue, I may conjecture, was very little to your purpose & even tiresome to read & I am the more convinc'd of this as I was never favor'd with any Answer.

What prompted me to such a prolixious narrative was my dread of the consequences of these circumstances mention'd therein, that might have happen'd to me in such a Journey, as I had already experienc'd several unpalatable Effects of such a superficial agreement, and as I always communicate every thing to You with such frankness, which I hope you'll excuse if I do it with too much confidence.

When I wrote you last I believe I mention'd, amongst other things, how barely he [James Adam] kept me in cloaths abroad, and what a pityfull suit he order'd me this Summer. Not that I mind my cloaths so much, but every one wou'd expect geneel treatment from a Master that has serv'd him so many Years as I have now done, & with such attention. When we first spoke about my last suit, he propos'd to give me a stuff of Silk & Cotton, but instead of that & without ever acquainting me of the change, bought me a very coarse woollen stuff worn by the lowest Tradesmen, which I took very ill & resolv'd that it shou'd not pass without him having some sharp answers, be the consequence what it wou'd. So I ask'd him if he had seen the Stuff that was bought for my cloaths. He said, Yes, why did I ask. I told him I hardly believ'd that he wou'd propos'd to give me a Silk & Cotton Stuff, & to buy such a coarse Stuff as had never been worn upon my back. He reply'd that a Silken

Stuff wou'd become dear. I told him I did not expect any thing of Silk, but thought I might pretend to a Coarse Camblet at least. He said, as we were going to Greece that it was a little Matter how we went. I said that might be, but I saw no reason why I shoul'd be oblig'd to go so meanly in Rome, where every one goes remarkably Genteel. Then he said that a suit might serve two summers & that at least if not this Season, next Summer we wou'd be in Turkey & that the more we all went like Slovens it wou'd be the better, to which I answer'd that he might have order'd the lining of by Breeches a little finer without any risk of the Turks seeing them, for they were fitter to make sacks of to hold corn than to be lining to my breeches & that I was sure they wou'd prod me for many Days before the hardness went of them, to which & some other things that I said he cou'd give no answer, or a very insignificant one. And I had the more reason to speak in this manner as one of my fellow companions has his cloaths from Mr Adam in the same way as me, who in this Winter past had a fine new suit of cloth cloaths & a suit of good Camblet this Summer at first asking, and I am sure I attend to his Service as close if not closer than any one he has.

But this agreement of giving cloaths will now soon be at an end, & perhaps now he will behave better than time past as we are nearer returning home. This winter I intend to make a new demand for a cloth suit, but allowing that I were to obtain it at first asking I shall always conclude that he has none other attention for me than merely for his own ends & purposes, after what has past. Tho' our return home cannot now be at a great distance, we have never as yet enter'd into any kind of discourse how I am to be situated at our arrival, I know he intends to settle in London with his Brother, & I understand he proposes keeping me with him there, but I have not this from his own Mouth, nor have I any notion whether his proposals will suit with my present situation in Life, as it wou'd require a pretty handsome income to keep a Family in a genteel way in London. But at the same time, I cannot entertain the smallest thoughts of doing without him or his Brothers, well knowing my own incapacity, small fortune, want of Books & little hopes of Interest if something does not cast up that I cannot expect. If we were to make his proposals to me before our return, I intend to avoid coming to a final agreement before our Arrival. One of my reasons for this is that I imagine it may make him behave the better to me on the Road, and I don't intend ever to make a longer agreement at a time than for one Year.

During our stay abroad I have now got together several rough Sketches of Antiquitys which will be very usefull for my own Study if I get them home conceal'd from Mr Adam's Sight, for I know if he were to see them, I wou'd run a risk of his everlasting displeasure, tho' I do them in by-hours & even when I shou'd sleep. For I have seen examples like this, when one wou'd do good for themselves they lose his favour, tho' it can by no means encroach upon any of his property's.

About middle of last Month I saw the praemiums distributed to the Students of Painting, Sculpture & Architecture by St Luke's Academy here, which is done with great pomp. But the honor is not near so much thought of here as in Britain, and if a Student have good Interest he may obtain a praemium tho' of no great Merit, nor do the professors do great Justice to the Competitors.

Since I have wrote the above, I have yesterday rec'd a letter from Henny, being 12th October. I beg you'll be so good to tell her when you see her that she may expect a long Letter from me in about a fortnight hence.

I am, Dear sir, with true Esteem and regard, your most obedient humble Servant.

GEORGE RICHARDSON

Address: To Archbald Shiells Esq
at his house
Inverask
near Edinburgh
Gran Bretagna

ALASDAIR ROBERTS

James Smith and James Gibbs: Seminarians and Architects

James Smith was a leading Scottish architect of his day whose real importance, it has been recently argued, consisted of making a link between Andrea Palladio and English classical architecture of the eighteenth century. James Gibbs was a Scotsman who achieved a very large reputation in that sphere a generation later. An important link between the two is Colen Campbell, a third Scotsman who produced the first Vitruvius Britannicus. *Campbell knew both Smith and Gibbs but helped neither. All three came from north-east Scotland, where the principles of Knox's Reformation had struggled for acceptance, and Smith and Gibbs (at least) were brought up as Roman Catholics. Both went to Rome with the intention of becoming priests, where the unsatisfactory state of the Scots College diverted them towards architecture. Both were able to return to Britain with a knowledge of Italian architecture which was not shared by their contemporaries, and a hidden Catholicism which may have influenced their creativity.*

INTRODUCTION

James Smith (1647?–1731) and James Gibbs (1682–1754) merit joint consideration as Scottish architects with a wider British influence who shared a common, 'un-Scottish', religious culture. Both went to the Scots College Rome from the minority Catholic community of north-east Scotland. Conditions in that religious seminary discouraged the two future architects, each in his own generation: both lost the intention to become priests but gained enough from their time in Italy to build the foundations of outstanding architectural careers. Smith came from Forres on the Moray Firth, his father a burgess of the same name, while Gibbs was the son of an Aberdeen merchant. Chance took these two men to Rome during the culminating period of its renaissance in stone, but when one considers how few Scots Catholics there were (perhaps five per cent of the population in 1680)[1] the religious dimension is remarkable. The very existence of a Scots College in Rome, enrolling scarcely fifty students in the period 1671–1704 which covers the attendance of Smith and Gibbs, was to make all the difference to Britain's architecture in the eighteenth century.

Smith is only now beginning to be seen as important figure, his name unrecorded in the international *Who's Who in Architecture* of 1977. Against a background of uncertainty as to whether Scottish builders of that generation were familiar with churches of the

Italian Renaissance, architectural historians have been unable to go beyond the suggestion that James Smith may have travelled in Europe, perhaps to Rome.[2] But it has been argued that this provincial overseer of royal buildings in Scotland (with little to oversee but Holyrood) played a key part in the genesis of British Palladianism:

> The use of Palladianism by James Smith was both more mature and more novel than anywhere else in Britain, a fact hitherto unrecognised by the generality of historians bemused by Scots Baronialism and the castles of the later sixteenth and seventeenth centuries in which, even a hundred years later, the great majority of landowners still lived.[3]

COLEN CAMPBELL

The fact that Smith's achievement has gone unrecognised for so long can be explained in a more particular way than the dominance, in historians' minds, of an earlier architectural style. Colen Campbell was a younger man but a more powerful one when it mattered, and it seems very likely that one Scotsman was able to exploit the talents of another:

> It is only in his surviving drawings that Smith's precocious interest in the architecture of Andrea Palladio can be demonstrated. There is evidence that these drawings passed into the possession of Colen Campbell, the leading publicist of English Palladianism, and reason to think that Campbell may have been in contact with Smith at the outset of his career as an architect. Certainly Smith's Palladian drawings appear to antedate any comparable drawings by Campbell or any other British architect of the eighteenth century.[4]

Colen Campbell (1676–1729) was the son of Donald Campbell, laird of Boghole five miles west of Forres, and must have known Smith's family from childhood. James Smith the father was a burgess of Forres, a master mason and a Roman Catholic. Campbell may also have begun life as a Catholic. A biographer has linked the architect's interest in repetitive geometrical forms to 'upbringing, a touch of prudent Scottish Calvinism',[5] but this may be dismissed as conjecture. On the other hand it is natural, given the leading role of the Argyll family in Whig politics, to assume that any Campbell would be presbyterian, and the architect's support for the established kirk is certainly implied by his sister's marriage to a minister. (The Rev. John Grant was no Calvinist, however. He was forced to resign his Auchinleck charge in 1731 after administering communion only twice in twenty years and scarcely ever visiting his parishioners.[6]) Three brothers of the Lochnell branch, on the north-western edge of the Campbell sphere of influence, came out strongly as Catholics in the early eighteenth century, one of them nearly becoming a vicar apostolic or bishop for the Highland district.[7]

Certain Campbells had been crypto-Catholics during the previous century. A letter was carried to the cardinal protector of the Scots College Rome in 1623 'per Coleno Campbello Scozzese',[8] although it was not until the following year that Campbell of

Calder received a Franciscan priest in his house at Muckairn in the district of Lochnell.[9] This was a west coast event. On the Moray Firth coast the house of Boghole appears to have been as significant as Muckairn. A John Gordon 'Boghollensis' was sent from the Scots College Paris to that of Douai, again in 1623.[10] There is nothing remarkable about a Gordon attending these Catholic seminaries, but the fact that Boghole was given to Donald Campbell by his older brother Sir Hugh Campbell of Cawdor shortly before the birth of the former's son Colen, the future architect, suggests a latent Catholicism in this branch of the family as well.

The main 'papisticall country'[11] of northern Scotland was in the parishes of Bellie and Rathven (to the east of Forres). Tenants were encouraged to be Catholics by the Gordons, whose Marquis of Huntly became Duke of Gordon under Charles II. North-east Scotland as a whole was slow to accept the Reformation, although the majority of disaffected gentry preferred the king's episcopalian compromise to 'popery'.

Campbell's unacknowledged borrowing of Smith's ideas has already been noted. The omission of James Gibbs' early work from Campbell's *Vitruvius Britannicus* looks like a similar act of professional sabotage, with religion the linking factor. Having achieved through fellow-lawyers a position of considerable power in London, Campbell seems to have used his familiarity with northern Catholicism to lean on Smith and Gibbs (one older, one younger) who learned that their secret was not safe with him. In a letter to the Church Commissioners of 13 January 1716 protesting at his dismissal Gibbs mentioned 'a false report of a Countrayman of mine that misrepresented me as a papest annd dissaffected person, which I can assure you is entirely false and scandalous, and done purly out of a designe to have gott himself into the place I have now lost'.[12] Campbell visited Rome himself in the first decade of the eighteenth century,[13] although not as a student of the Scots College. The most interesting section of this paper is probably on the experience of Smith and Gibbs in that institution, but first it may be helpful to place them as architects.

SMITH THE ARCHITECT

When James Smith went from Forres to Rome (perhaps with the encouragement of Colen Campbell's father) and entered the Scots College in 1671 he was expected to return as a priest four years later. The college register states that he formally renounced the Catholic faith ('factus est apostata'[14]) but this must have taken place some time after he left—without being ordained—in 1675.

On his return from Rome Smith's career was given the best of starts when he became a burgess of Edinburgh in 1679 by right of his marriage to the elder daughter of Robert Mylne, the king's master mason.[15] James Smith was to become the father of thirty-two children—by two wives—despite his boyhood resolve for celibacy.[16] The Mylnes formed a dynasty of Scottish builders from the sixteenth century to the eighteenth, and the family's influence spread to England in the 1760s through Robert Mylne.[17] Smith rose quickly to become overseer of the King's Works under the Catholic James Duke of York, who has received recent attention as a patron of the arts during his 1679–1682 period in Edinburgh.[18] York succeeded his brother Charles in 1685 as James VII and II, and Smith's position remained secure. When Holyrood Abbey was briefly given over to Catholic worship (and to the Order of the Thistle which James created) as the Chapel Royal, a new church was built in the Canongate for its congregation. The architect's religious affiliation was noted by the church's minister-historian:

> He was (and perhaps was chosen by design) a Roman Catholic, which may help to explain the unique cruciform plan, almost Jesuit in character. Dutch influence is also evident. The interior, 'with its arcade of simple classical columns supporting semi-circular arches, its transepts and spacious sanctuary ending in an apse with a curious contemporary Gothic window, is quite unlike anything else built in Scotland at the time and is far more akin to Continental practice'.[19]

The building has been described as 'more appropriate to the needs of a Jesuit "mass-house"' than those of a seventeenth-century parish kirk',[20] and the editor of this journal discerns a specifically Italian influence, its lobed facade typical of many Venetian Gothic parish churches. Whatever the building's inspiration, the shield of Nassau in the royal arms on the main gable of the Canongate Kirk links it with the accession of William of Orange: Smith must have formally renounced his Catholic faith soon after the Revolution of 1688, in order to keep his post under the new government.

His own house at Newhailes was completed during James's short reign, and (as if to illustrate altered political allegiance) a version of the same design was used for Melville House, home of the Whig president of the Privy Council at the turn of the eighteenth century.[21] Smith's other buildings include Dalkeith Palace and also Yester House and church at Gifford in East Lothian—a link with the Canongate Kirk, since the site belonged to Lady Yester. Smith was described in Campbell's *Vitruvius Britannicus* as 'the most experienc'd architect' in Scotland.[22] Despite the formal renunciation he continued a secret Catholic. This may be assumed from his association with the Stewarts of Traquair, whose 'Popish wares' were burned at the market cross of Peebles during the Revolution,[23] and James Smith died a 'reputed Roman Catholic' in 1731.[24]

GIBBS THE ARCHITECT

The religious allegiance of James Gibbs can also be considered in relation to his career. He too was under pressure to commit himself to the Protestant establishment, particularly in 1713 when he became responsible for building fifty London churches. This was under Queen Anne, but circumstances changed when the Elector of Hanover became George I: 'His career was complicated by his Catholic faith and Tory politics; he suffered from the disapproval of the Whig government, being dismissed from his Surveyorship of the Church Building Commission'.[25] This 1716 dismissal taught Gibbs that Catholicism had to be concealed, but it is ironic that his union of traditional steeple with classical temple at St Martin-in-the-Fields was to be 'one of the most original and influential achievements of English Protestant church architecture'.[26]

In the final settling of his affairs Gibbs arranged for masses to be said for his soul by priests of the Scottish mission: Father Alexander Grant (who knew him as a neighbour in Soho) considered Gibbs niggardly in these mass stipends. He died a wealthy man in 1754, and it cannot have been for the actual value of a £150 annual pension that he kept his Catholic allegiance 'under a mask'.[27] During the latter part of his life Gibbs corresponded with a 'Father Peters' (Francis Petre became bishop in the north of England two years before Gibbs' death[28]) who was his spiritual director and gave him 'the last rites of his principles'.[29] The Gibbs library was mainly stocked with books on building (including his own influential *Book of Architecture* of 1728) but it also provides evidence on his beliefs:

> The religious collection is consistent with a life divided between two per-
> suasions . . . No missal, apparently, was among the books, but Mass books
> were more dangerous possessions in those days than Douai Bibles, and if
> Gibbs possessed one he may have parted with it in private . . . It seems,
> from what else we know of his prosperous days, that Gibbs long found the
> burden of open Catholicism, or even crypto-Catholicism, too much to
> bear and far too much of an impediment to his ambition and fondness for
> worldly comfort. At the end, it seems, in those last years of leisure and of
> assured, unambitious ease, he cautiously returned, with a priest to see him
> in his own home and Egan his Irish servant to guard the door, to the
> religion whose altars he had once intended to serve.[30]

THE SCOTS COLLEGE ROME

Having established that James Smith and James Gibbs both found it necessary to dissemble their Catholic faith, we may now consider their experiences of Rome. The *Collegio Scozzese* there had been established in the opening years of the seventeenth century near the Trevi fountain. In 1646 the Church of St Andrew of the Scotsmen, built with funds provided by the Marchioness of Huntly, became a chapel for the students. Queen Henrietta Maria lent money to provide a new wing overlooking the Via Rasella, and by the time Smith arrived it had become customary to spend the hottest months of summer at the college's vineyard at Marino. The revenue from sales of wine was important to the economy of the institution—always uncertain despite benefactions, from popes down to quite humble people: 'One donation of money is surely unique in the history of colleges. In 1657 the cook, Claud Riel, left to the Scots College the savings which he had accumulated in its service'.[31] By the end of the seventeenth century the library, formed largely by the donations of parting rectors, included nearly two thousand books and about fifty manuscripts.

When James Smith entered the Scots College in 1671 it had just been placed under its first Italian rector in half a century. Father Marini was in post from February 1671 to March 1674, and according to one outspoken critic he 'governed so very ill and occasioned such disturbances that scarcely a student choosed to remain under him'.[32] Seventeenth century students (as distinct from their successors of the eighteenth) were commonly men in their twenties like Smith, and it was his misfortune to coincide with a first—rather crude—attempt at improving discipline:

> At first no special clauses were made about crimes for which students
> must be expelled. However in 1671 an attempt was made to tabulate them
> in the following list: drunkenness, striking another student, rebellion
> against the rector, failure to pass examinations . . . The list was modified,
> both in 1676 and 1681. Drunkenness remained, but striking must be
> without provocation, rebellion must be pertinacious, failure to pass exami-
> nations must be notable before the student could be expelled . . . The
> disciplined life of the College seems to have been irksome at times to the
> young Scotsmen . . . Penance 'chits' . . . give a good picture of the
> rowdiness which must often have astonished the Jesuit superiors.
> Sometimes the offender has missed one of the classes at the University, at
> another time he has obtained leave to go to the basilicas, and has gone for
> a walk instead.[33]

As James Smith walked to his university classes and to the basilicas he would have worn the college's distinctive dress: 'Violet soutane, red cincture and a black soprana—a sleeveless overgarment, open at the front, with long narrow bands of cloth, which are conventionalised sleeves, hanging from the shoulders . . . an inheritance from the medieval Scottish Hospice in Rome'.[34]

The most obvious point to make about students like Smith and Gibbs is that they were a long way from home. During the latter's time a fellow student was reprieved by Pope Clement XI for having sworn at the rector: 'He would not suffer a boy to come heir the length of a thousand and five hundred miles and then be thrown out for one word'.[35] A typical journey from Scotland might include a voyage from Aberdeen to Holland and a stay in the Scots College Paris, where expenses or 'viatick' for the remainder of the journey would be arranged. Letters between these institutions provide glimpses of students coming and going—in Smith's case the briefest reference to his returning home in November 1675: 'If I did not dayly expect to hear particularly from you by Mr Smith, who as wee hear is on his journey for Paris, I should with reason complain of your silence'.[36]

Sometimes the stay at Paris on the way home would be an extended one, for the Rome course was of a general nature and gave scant consideration to the particular problems of a missionary priest in Scotland. Regardless of whether the visitor was an ordained cleric or a disenchanted ex-student there would often be commiserations over conditions in the Roman college. The two institutions represented alternative views on how the Scottish mission should be supplied with priests. From Archbishop Beaton's time through to the Jacobite court in exile at St Germain, Paris was more Scottish in emphasis, and committed to the view that 'secular' clergy (diocesan priests until the Reformation, belonging to no religious order) were what was needed, under ecclesiastical superiors equivalent to bishops. Secular clergy ran the Paris college, as distinct from the Jesuit control of the other Scots colleges at Rome, Douai and Madrid, while a fifth source of priests for Scotland, the south German monasteries of Ratisbon and Würzburg, strengthened the influence of 'regular' clergy who lived by rule—in their case the rule of St Benedict. The point is worth clarifying because the tension between regulars and seculars was to be the main thing which dissuaded both Smith and Gibbs from completing their course of training.

The Society of Jesus, founded in the sixteenth century for purposes of conversion and Counter-Reformation, was a world-wide organisation with a particular concern for education. The Jesuits believed that the way to achieve their religious aims was through a highly educated clergy, obedient to superiors and capable of being deployed anywhere as the changing needs of the Church required. Resources were always stretched, however, and Scotland's bursts of strong commitment to the Reformation made it sensible, on occasion, to use Scottish priests elsewhere. Secular priests objected to the way Jesuit superiors tried to persuade the brightest of the students at their Scots colleges to transfer to the order and its longer course of training. They were able to persuade Rome's ecclesiastical authorities, through the *Congregatio de Propaganda Fide*, to require a 'mission oath' of students. This had been tightened in 1660 so that seminarians had to give an undertaking soon after their enrolment that they would return to the Scottish mission as secular priests—and stay there: the former oath had merely stipulated a three-year period in Scotland. Thus the 'fecit juramentum' which appears in the register for most students.

SMITH THE SEMINARIAN

The first of two entries for 1671 reads *Jacobus Smith Moraviensis. Fecit juramentum 3 Maii; studuit rhet. an. 1, phil. 3, Theol. 1. 3 Octobris 1675 discessit cum licentia Protectoris et promissione redeundi sed factus est apostata.*: 'James Smith of Moray diocese took the oath on 3 May; he studied rhetoric for one year, philosophy for three years and theology for one year. He left on 3 October 1675 with the Protector's permission and with a promise of returning, but formally renounced the Catholic faith'.[37] A six-month settling in period was normal, so Smith may be assumed to have reached Rome late in 1670. Just before he took the oath Robert Munro set off for what proved to be over thirty years of dedicated service in the Highlands. On the other hand Robert Douglas left without being ordained in the year of Smith's arrival, and Thomas Strachan was only in college for a year with him before taking up a military career in Germany. But the records do not altogether support the charge that Fr. Marini 'governed so very ill . . . that scarcely a student choosed to remain under him'. David Guthrie and Robert Davidson arrived from the diocese of St Andrews in 1672 and stayed the course, as did Alexander Christie and William Douglas in 1674. And John Irvine, who was to feature in the dispute which persuaded Smith to return to Scotland, was a month junior to him. Irvine survived the College's difficulties and went on to become a leading figure on the mission as chaplain to the Duke of Gordon.

Despite Marini's reputation it was to be a Scottish rather than an Italian rector who provoked the significant crisis soon after his appointment in March 1674. This was William Lewis Leslie of Balquhain (by Fetternear in Aberdeenshire) who emphasised his Jesuit commitment by using the Aloysius version of Lewis. Middle names are important here, because he was to be opposed by another William Leslie, a cousin, on behalf of the secular clergy of Scotland. 'Dom Guilielmo' or Will Leslie has been described as 'a personage of greater influence in the Roman ecclesiastical world of the second half of the 17th century than many Cardinals'.[38] During more than half a century as Roman agent of the Scottish mission his suspicion of the Jesuits was such that he has been credited with the almost single-handed destruction of their mission to China. However that may be, he was quick to respond to a report from John Irvine that the new rector had told the Scots students under his charge that 'the oath as prohibiting of a greater good was essentially null and unlawful. So much did he cavil on this . . . that he nearly succeeded in turning the heads of the four students of which the college then consisted and persuading them to join the society'.[39]

The historian Abbé Paul MacPherson is suggesting here that the future architect nearly became a Jesuit priest, which would imply a strong degree of commitment. MacPherson reported that three of the students, including Smith, were persuaded by the rector's arguments, although Irvine told Will Leslie that he was concerned about the sin of perjury. The Agent replied immediately promising a full and reasoned argument to follow ('nine sheets of large paper and small character', as it turned out) but meanwhile he urged the students 'to suspend their judgement on a matter of such weight and not think of forsaking their vocation till they had heard and examined what he had to say as well as what the Rector had urged'.[40] We may assume that James Smith read the full document in his turn and that discussions took place among the students on the moral imperatives being put to them from both sides. Favourably impressed by Will Leslie's paper (and by John Irvine) they reached their decision:

> The young men, ashamed of their own inadvertency and simplicity, were
> enraged at the cunning and, as they now termed it, criminal attempt of
> the Rector to mislead them, much to their own ruin and prejudice of
> their country. They bitterly reproached him to his face for the ungenerous

use he made of the confidence they reposed in him, and the base advantage he took of their inexperience. So far did they allow the spirit of resentment to hurry them that scarcely could they show common civility to their superior. [However] the Agent, informed by the students' letter of their temper and present disposition, wrote them another long letter in which he strongly censures their behaviour to their superior. You think, says he, your Rector has acted wrong, and in this you think not amiss, but whence are your powers of calling him to account derived? Who authorised you to punish him? His motives and intention . . . may in his opinion have been lawful and even laudable . . . He is your lawful superior; in that capacity by the express and often-repeated law of God without any possible restriction he has a just title to your respect on all occasions; and to your obedience in every lawful command.[41]

Dom Guilielmo went on in the same way for another two sheets (it is easy to see why he was nicknamed the Homilist) creating such a state of psychological confusion in the minds of his readers, we may surmise, that it is surprising James Smith was the only student to quit the seminary. Even so he left with a promise to return and the approval of Cardinal Barberini, whose palace overlooked the Scots College. As its designated Protector he no doubt sympathised with the young man. We know that Smith left Italy almost at once, heading for Paris and Scotland. What remains unclear, however, is how he acquired his knowledge of Andrea Palladio. A letter has survived which may cast partial light on the question. It was written to John Irvine by his cousin Christopher, a medical student at Padua, some four months before Smith's student career came to an unexpected end. Most of the following extract is included for its account of Italian student life:

The University is a little deminished be what it was att my coming, the most part of the studens [sic] are retourned homeward already, so that there is few schollars heere att present except for strangers or citisans of Padua, so that I enjoy att present a little more liberty, for at [illegible] heere there was a great feodge between the schollars of Vicenza and those of Br [illegible] and there confederats, they ware about thrie hundred a syd all armed with carrabins and a paire of pistoles by there syds, there was no passing through the streets without danger, they did kill severall that they imagined to be there adversairs, the podesta att last with much adoo did agree them, yet they ware allways diffident of on an other, and for that reason retourned home sonner than the ordinaire, our cheife study now is the simples, which will continoue to the latter end of May and then the vacance beginnes. Present my service to Mr Smith and show him that those of Vicenza in this quarrell was worsted, two of there faction being killed, and the rest constrained to keep there loggings.[42]

Vicenza was the city of Andrea Palladio, where he had designed a number of public buildings in the sixteenth century. The letter seems to establish a link between the two architects, assuming that the same Mr. Smith is involved, but it is hard to believe that

Smith would have been permitted to visit Vicenza while a student in Rome at a time
when the rector was trying to limit walks to a small area of the city. It is more likely
that the young Scotsman had earlier travelled Europe with a sketch pad: if he encountered Palladio's work in Vicenza before entering the college it could be said that he gave
up architecture for religion, in the first instance. James Smith probably re-visited
Vicenza on his journey to Paris. He was established in Edinburgh by 1679, where his
Roman experience and Catholicism must have helped him win favour with the Duke of
York. Four years later, while still in his thirties, he succeeded William Bruce, the
leading Scottish architect of his day, as overseer or surveyor of the royal works in
Scotland.[43]

GIBBS THE SEMINARIAN

The case of James Gibbs is not so very different, since the Scots College was in a similar
state of uproar during his short time there from October 1703 to August 1704. Gibbs'
background and early life have already been well documented.[44] The family name in
Scotland was Gibb rather than Gibbs.[45] James's father Patrick or Peter Gibb was a
merchant living close to the port of Aberdeen at Links of Fittie's Myre and trading with
Holland. Aberdeen was the only Scottish town with a sizeable community of Catholics
(perhaps four hundred) and merchants like Gibb and his brother Alexander made
common cause with the gentry families of Menzies, Irvine and Leslie who lived outside
the city. They had been confident during the short reign of James Stuart and were
inclined to be defiant at its sudden end:

> At the Revolution of 1688, party feeling running high, old Mr Gibbs, who
> was a Roman Catholic, named two dogs he had Calvin and Luther in
> derision of both Presbyterians and Episcopalians. For this the magistrates
> of Aberdeen summoned him to appear before them and sagaciously
> ordered the offending puppies to be hanged.[46]

It was in the home of Alexander Gibb ten years later that a mass was interrupted by the
same magistrates, the householder and two others being sent to prison in Edinburgh
'with all their Popish trinkets'.[47] The fifteen-year-old who was shortly to try his vocation
as a priest may very well have served as an altar boy on that occasion. At a later date
Scottish churchmen abroad were concerned to help James Gibbs because of 'his father
having suffered much for the faith at the revolution'.[48] Despite the family's noncon-
formity Gibbs received a good education at Aberdeen's grammar school and at Marischal
College, his university studies covering the period 1696–1700 although he did not
graduate.

Whether on account of the uncongenial atmosphere in Scotland or simply because of
a 'rambling disposition . . . to see other countries',[49] the young Gibbs went to Holland
after leaving university and stayed with an aunt at Veere. He made a rather slow progress
towards Italy by way of Flanders, Paris, Switzerland and Vienna, no doubt exercising his

'great genius to drawing'[50] on the way. Gibbs' most recent biographer makes the point that France was inaccessible to his Protestant countrymen in the war years prior to the Treaty of Utrecht.[51] His age on entering the Scots College Rome is recorded with precision: 'James Gibb, son of Patrick Gibb of Fittsmyre and Anne Gordon of Aberdeen, twenty-one and a half years old, entered the college on 12 October 1703'.[52] Like Smith, he arrived at an unfortunate time. Fr. William Leslie's second stint as rector had been followed by that of another Scot, James Forbes (1695–1702) but Gibbs' short period in college was to coincide with the rule of two Italian rectors who, 'not knowing our people's genius, use ways quite contrary to their humour and nature that the best and most hopeful youths are like to be forced away or leave of themselves'.[53]

Dom Guilielmo Leslie was still keeping a watchful eye on the troubled Scots College, although the oath had ceased to be a problem (except, as it turned out, for James Gibbs) and only one student had joined the Jesuits since Smith's time. Secular criticism of Jesuit rectors now extended to their refusal to accept all of the eight students for which the college was funded, poor feeding of those who were admitted, peculation of funds, failure to provide training in pastoral work, and harshness to students. The first of the Italians was Didacus Calcagni, 'a violent hot-headed old man void of every qualification to govern youth . . . During three whole years Calcagni governed the college with the most despotic tyranny; at one stroke he swept away all the ancient rules and constitutions'.[54]

Calcagni was replaced three months after Gibbs' arrival by Fr Giovanni Naselli, but 'the change of rectors brought little relief to the students . . . In lieu of an old tyrant the General had sent them a young one, who besides continuing the barbarities of his predecessor was so base as to inflict his penances with blows'.[55] A particular dispute involving one of the 'ancient rules and constitutions' (the right to invite students from the English College for the feast of St Margaret of Scotland on 10th June) led to the expulsion of the most outspoken student.[56] Long before that occurred the most recent arrival was being actively discouraged from any thoughts of a priestly vocation by his rector, if we are to believe Will Leslie:

> Poor Mr Gib who came in last is so terrified with his rudeness that he cannot resolve to take the oath; he should have taken it months ago but then the rector did not tender it to him, and he has been in such broils since that he won't go under it at any rate. The truth is the Rector, besides the hardships he gives them frequently to swallow, does directly dishearten them all from following out their obligations, telling them that though they now be desirous to take orders 'tis like they come to repent it when they have taken them.[57]

Naselli's version appears in the register: 'He refused to take the oath. He had twice been given permission to put off the time . . . yet he refused to take it'.[58] James Gibbs handed back his soutane, cincture and soprana in August 1705. He was able to stay on in Rome thanks to a loan of one hundred crowns from James Gordon, Leslie's deputy, who commented: 'The youth is of good parts and vertuously inclined and well disposed, and though he leave the college may be usefull one day . . . He resolves to stay some while here and apply himself to painting, seemingly to have a great genious for that employ-ment'.[59] In fact the mass stipends mentioned earlier were the only tangible use that the Scottish mission ever had of him.

   Gibbs soon gave up the idea of being a painter, although he was to leave his last house to an Aberdeen artist, Cosmo John Alexander, who was a Catholic and fought at Culloden. Gibbs' first biographer suggests that he was not a serious church student, and his degree of commitment certainly seems to have been less than that of Smith: 'He may never, indeed, have had a really strong bent towards the priesthood . . . Nor does he seem for some time to have finally decided that architecture was to be his final occupation. Now, however, with his college days behind him and with funds to start him on his way, he was free to take stock of the scenes and possibilities of Rome in the last years of its great Baroque phase'.[60] Accepted into the school of Carlo Fontana, Rome's leading architect after Bernini, Gibbs used his time well until 1708, when the illness of a brother brought him home—but only as far as London. The Earl of Mar (an amateur architect of some distinction whom Gibbs had met in Holland) proved a helpful patron, but truly the young architect had much to offer on his own account.

CONCLUSION

Gibbs offered the same scarce commodity as James Smith: an unexpected familiarity with Italian architecture at a time when Britain was moving out of a long period of religious tumult and into the age of reason. Unfortified buildings of great style, including Protestant churches, were to be one of the expressions of that age. It is a paradox that early 18th-century English architecture was advanced by two men who were nurtured in a culture of religious extremism, relative to the dominant Calvinism of Scotland. Genius views its task from an unusual angle. As employees of the Protestant state both Smith and Gibbs were forced to abandon at least the public profession of their faith but maintained, in differing ways, a private practice. Any attempt to establish a single argument on the basis of two unique individuals from different generations is liable to fall, but the sheer strangeness of leaving a minority Scottish Catholic community in order to pursue a priestly vocation in so disturbed an institution as the Scots College Rome may be persuasive in this case. Neither could have ever quite forgotten their first vocations and their traumatic experience as church students. Out of what amounted to the same impossible situation the two seminarians changed their minds. They came home as architects.

REFERENCES

1. J. Darragh, 'The Catholic population of Scotland since the year 1680', *Innes Review*, **4**, 1953.

2. G. Hay, *The Architecture of Scottish Post-Reformation Churches, 1560–1843*, Oxford, 1957, pp. 65, 67; J. Macaulay, *The Classical Country House in Scotland, 1660–1800*, London, 1987, p. 27.

3. Macaulay, *op. cit.*, p. 51.

4. H.M. Colvin, 'James Smith', in A.K. Placzek, *The MacMillan Encyclopaedia of Architecture*, London, 1982, vol. 4, pp. 89–90. See also Colvin, 'A Scottish origin for English Palladianism?' in *Architectural History*, 17, 1974, pp. 5–13; Colvin, *A Bibliographical Dictionary of British Architects*, London, 1954, p. 119; J. Summerson, *Architecture in Britain, 1530 to 1830*. 5th ed., 1969, p. 197.

5. C. Saumarez Smith, Colin Campbell, in Placzek, *op. cit.*, 1982, vol. 1, p. 368.

6. H. Scott, *Fasti Ecclesiae Scoticanae: the Succession of Ministers in Scotland since the Reformation*, Vol. 3, Edinburgh, 1920, p. 3.

7. J.F. McMillan, 'Jansenists and anti-Jansenists in eighteenth-century Scotland: the *Unigenitus* quarrels of the Scottish Catholic Mission', *Innes Review*, **39**, 12–45.

8. Letter to Cardinal Barberini, 1623, catalogued Barb[erini] Lat[eran] 8629 (Scots College Rome) in the Vatican Library and copied in the Scottish Catholic Archives, Drummond Place, Edinburgh, p. 68v.

9. C. Giblin, *Irish Franciscan Mission to Scotland 1619–1646*, Dublin, 1964, p. 53.

10. *Records of the Scots Colleges at Rome, Madrid, Valladolid and Ratisbon*, Aberdeen, 1906, p. 15.

11. J.F.S. Gordon, *The Catholic Church in Scotland*, Aberdeen, 1874, p. 2.

12. T. Friedman, *James Gibbs*, New Haven & London, 1984, p. 10.

13. Colvin, *op. cit.*, 1974, p. 13.

14. *Records of Scots Colleges*, p. 118.

15. J.G. Dunbar, quoted in Colvin, *op. cit.*, 1974, p. 8.

16. J.G. Dunbar, *The Historic Architecture of Scotland*, London, 1966, p. 101.

17. A.F. Richardson, *Robert Mylne, Architect and Engineer, 1733 to 1811*, London, 1955.

18. H. Ouston, 'York in Edinburgh: James VII and the patronage of learning in Scotland, 1679–1688', Dwyer, J. et al. (eds.), *New Perspectives on the Politics and Culture of Early Modern Scotland*, Edinburgh, 1980; *idem*, 'Cultural life from the Restoration to the Union', Hook, A. (ed.), *The History of Scottish Literature*, Vol. 2. Aberdeen, 1987.

19. R. Selby Wright, *The Kirk in the Canongate*, Edinburgh, 1956, p. 79.

20. Hay, *op. cit.*, p. 67.

21. J. Gifford, *The Buildings of Scotland: Fife*, London, 1988, p. 46.

22. C. Campbell, *Vitruvius Britannicus or the British Architect*, 1715–25, Vol. 2, p. 3.

23. O. Blundell, *Ancient Catholic Homes of Scotland*, London, 1907, p. 132.

24. Dunbar, *op. cit.*, p. 101.

25. J.M. Richards, *Who's Who in Architecture from 1400 to the Present Day*. London, 1977, p. 118.

26. Placzek, *op. cit.*, vol. 2, p. 197.

27. Letter from Alexander Grant (London) to Bishop Alexander Smith (Edinburgh) 31 August 1754. *Blairs Letters*, Edinburgh: Scottish Catholic Archives.

28. J. Bossy, *The English Catholic Community, 1570–1850*, London, 1975, p. 213.

29. Grant, *loc. cit.*

30. B. Little, *The Life and Work of James Gibbs, 1682–1754*, London, 1955, pp. 164, 162.

31. W.E. Brown, 'Essay on the history of the Scots College', *The Scots College Rome*. London, 1930, pp. 12, 16.

32. W.J. Anderson, 'Abbe Paul MacPherson's History of the Scots College, Rome', *Innes Review*, **12**, 1961, p. 39.

33. Brown, *op. cit.*, p. 10.

34. D.R. McRoberts, 'Scots College, Rome: students' dress', *Innes Review*, **2**, 1951, p. 113.

35. A. Roberts, 'Gregor, McGregor (1681–1740) and the Highland problem in the Scottish Catholic mission', *Innes Review*, **39**, 1988, p. 86.

36. Lewis Innes (Paris) to John Irvine (Rome) 8 November 1675. *Blairs Letters*.

37. *Records of the Scots Colleges*, p. 118.

38. M. Hay, *Failure in the Far East*, London, 1956, p. 19.

39. Anderson, *op. cit.*, p. 40.

40. *Ibid.*, p. 41.

41. *Ibid.*, p. 48–9.

42. Christopher Irvine (Padua) to John Irvine (Rome) 16 April 1675. *Blairs Letters*.

43. Dunbar, *op. cit.*, p. 101.

44. A.S. MacWilliam, James Gibbs, architect, 1682–1754, *Innes Review*, **5**, 1954, pp. 101–3; Little, *op. cit.*

45. *Scottish Notes and Queries*, 1901, pp. 110, 131.

46. W. Anderson, *The Scottish Nation*, Edinburgh, 1862, pp. 294.

47. A. Bellesheim, *History of the Catholic Church of Scotland*, Edinburgh, 1989, p. 143.

48. James Gordon (Rome) to Lewis Innes (Paris) 19 August 1704, *Blairs Letters*.

49. Soane MS, quoted in Little, *op. cit.*, p. 7.

50. *Ibid.*

51. Friedman, *op. cit.*, p. 5.

52. *Record of Scots Colleges*, p. 126.

53. William Leslie (Rome) to Lewis Innes (Paris) 29 July 1704. *Blairs Letters.*

54. Anderson, *op. cit.*, pp. 94, 96.

55. *Ibid.*, p. 97.

56. Roberts, *op. cit.*

57. William Leslie (Rome) to Lewis Innes (Paris) 12 August 1705. *Blairs Letters.*

58. *Record of Scots Colleges*, p. 126.

59. James Gordon (Rome) to Lewis Innes (Paris) 19 August 1705. *Blairs Letters.*

60. Little, *op. cit.*, p. 15.

SOPHIE DRINKALL

The Jamaican Plantation House: Scottish Influence

Jamaica, from the late seventeenth to the early nineteenth century, was one of Britain's most lucrative colonies. The wealth of the island was created by two industries: sugar and, later, coffee. Their business interests established, their large and imposing processing works, aqueducts, mills, boiling and curing houses built, the more prosperous plantation owners turned their attention to building increasingly substantial and interesting homes. Jamaica's greatest architectural glory lies in these plantation buildings.

WHEN the foundations of the earliest Jamaican plantation houses were being laid at the beginning of the eighteenth century, the influence of Andrea Palladio was the height of fashion in Britain, the mother country. This same influence was to dominate the architecture of colonial Jamaica over a period of almost two hundred years. The style evolved gradually until by the middle of the nineteenth century it had become what T.A.L. Concannon saw as a 'recognisable Jamaican vernacular' with numerous distinguishing features: louvered windows, projecting louvered window 'coolers', pitched shingle roofs, simple decorative fretwork eaves, bargeboards and balcony railings. This article will attempt to identify some of the contributions Scotsmen made in influencing the evolution of this distinct architectural form.

Although the island had been discovered by the Spanish in the late fifteenth century, it was the British, arriving in Jamaica in 1655, who made the island's colonisation effective. The initial problems the early colonists faced in making their investments viable were enormous. Encouraging new settlers to come and work the plantations required immense persuasion or, failing that, brute force. The failure of the 1654 Highland uprising against Cromwell made Scotland an obvious source of cheap manpower for the island: Scottish rebels became the first of many indentured servants to till Jamaican soil. The request for their labour came on July 18th 1655. Major General Richard Fortescue, of the Company of General Venables which had conquered the island, sent a petition of 'Several considerations to be humbly represented to his Highness the Lord Protector & Council, in behalf of the army in America'. One of Fortescue's proposals was that

> several from Scotland or elsewhere, may be sent to assist in planting, for which the officers out of their pay will make such allowance as his Highness shall think fit, and assign them such proportions of land as his Highness shall direct at the expiration of their respective terms.[1]

The response, as Edward Long reported in his *History of Jamaica* (1774), was decisive and prompt:

> the Protector ordered the Council of Scotland to command the sheriffs of the several counties, the commissioners of parishes, and heritors of lands, that they should apprehend all known, idle, masterless robbers and vagabonds, male and female, and transport them to that island . . .[2]

Having served their term, bonded servants were free to seek employment wherever they chose. Their lives were certainly hard and little better than those of the negroes alongside whom they worked, but inspite of such hardship these enforced immigrants were to achieve much in Jamaica.

One of the more successful groups of these indentured or bonded servants owed their arrival in Jamaica to the disastrously ill-fated Scottish venture to colonise the isthmus at Darien. The evident potential of this settlement so threatened jealous English merchants—in particular those that had invested in the East India Company—that they set out to obstruct its development from the start. It was not long before they had managed to pervert the aims of this Scottish enterprise to the extent that William III himself intervened in 1699 and thwarted the initiative.[3]

A handful of the Scots refugees from Darien did survive, raising themselves out of the mire, making a success of their enormous misfortunes. To circumvent the legislation that had been passed unjustly against them, the majority of Darien's survivors chose to commit themselves to a period of indentured service. At the end of their term, most of these men of fortitude went on not only to accumulate a share in Jamaica's burgeoning prosperity but also to attain some of the island's most cherished positions of public office. Even if those that had subscribed to the Darien venture were of varied background and ranged from craftsmen to aristocrats, in common they held an astonishing desire to succeed despite adversities.

Compassion for the stranded and isolated Darien survivors persuaded the authorities to allow the Scots to establish themselves along the west coast of the island, in the parish of Westmoreland. Here the names they chose for their settlements, such as Scot's Cave, Auchindown and Culloden, clearly reflect both their origins and the bitterness they felt at their treatment by the English. According to Long the area was prone to high winds and heavy rains though the ground was very fertile and suitable for the production of sugar.

In 1745 Scotsmen constituted one quarter of the island's landholders and by Edward Long's day nearly one third of the island's population were of Scottish descent:

> I heard a computation made of no fewer than one hundred of the name of Campbel, . . . all claiming alliance with the Argyle family . . .[4]

A Colonel Campbell is one of those cited by Charles Leslie as a successful Darien survivor. Archbald, Earl of Argyle, also heads the 1696 list of subscribers to the

Company of Scotland which funded the Darien venture.[5] Yet there is no evidence for a direct familial link between these and, for instance, the two Campbells who owned the estates of Copse, Beverley and New Milnes in the parish of Hanover.

Just as it is difficult to establish the link between estate owners of the same name, so is it to ascribe names of specific Scottish craftsmen to the building work carried out upon these plantations. Nonetheless, we do know that Scotsmen were imported particularly and trained for this purpose. In 1740, for instance, Sir James Campbell of Auchinbreck set up a scheme to transport such labour to the island. In 1794, as a direct result of this scheme, one Alexander Monteith settled in Jamaica as a master carpenter. Long is full of admiration for these immigrants:

> The artificers, particularly stone-masons and mill-wrights, from that part of Britain, are remarkably expert, and in general are sober, frugal and civil; the good education which the poorest of them receive, having great influence on their morals and behaviour.[6]

If the names of these Scottish artisans are illusive, and the patrons behind them somewhat difficult to place, the plantation buildings themselves certainly reveal their origins and inspirations: both in their estate names and in the form of the structures, the links with Scotland are undeniable.

Primarily for effect but also for security, the great house of a plantation tended to be built on high ground and well away from the noise of the estate's agricultural buildings. The houses were handsomely jalousied on the more peaceful plantations but were necessarily strongly loopholed on those estates which saw frequent slave revolts. An excellent example of one of Jamaica's more fortified estate houses is Stewart's Castle, near Auckendown, the area designated to the survivors of Darien (Fig. 1). It is believed to have been built around 1770, long after the serious threat of raids and rebellions had receded. Little remains of the building today but its ruins and descriptions of the estate suggest a parallel in Colbeck Castle, built for military purposes on the south side of the island (Fig. 2). Here the loopholed ruined walls probably stood at a height of about thirty feet. The most notable features of this stronghold are the four corner towers, each three stories high, built of grey stone with quoins and window reveals of brick. A reversal of the usual treatment, this is probably due to the scarcity of brick in Jamaica: with local supplies inadequate, brick was imported from Britain as ballast on ships that would return to Europe with cargoes of sugar. The towers are joined by a double range of arcaded brick loggias, four arches on the short sides and five on the long. Set into walls of stone filled in with rubble, the windows on the ground floor have brick quoins and window facings. The graceful tall arches that once linked the towers on the length of the castle opposite the entrance would surely seem to belie a purely military inspiration. Stewart's Castle is distinct from Colbeck only in its towers of which, unusually, there are only two, placed at diagonal corners. These two Jamaican buildings recall a strong

1. James Hakewill's view of Stewart's Castle Estate, c.1820. Built c.1770. (Institute of Jamaica)

2. Colbeck Castle, built c.1690, is an example of Jamaica's fortified corner tower buildings that were inspired by a strong Scottish architectural tradition. (Jack Tyndale-Biscoe)

3. Now-demolished, Craighall in Fife, remodelled by William Bruce c. 1680, shows remarkable similarities to Jamaican corner tower plantation houses. (RCAHMS)

Scottish architectural tradition manifested especially in some of Bruce's work. The similarities of what remains of Colbeck Castle, compared to the photograph of the now-demolished Craighall (Fig. 3) in Fife, are remarkable. William Hope of Craighall is registered in the 'List of Subscribers to the Company of Scotland' as having invested five hundred pounds.[7]

Fortified buildings such as Stewart's Castle, however, stand outside the mainstream of Jamaica's architectural plantation house tradition. It soon became apparent that this style of construction was little suited to the environment of the colony. Although the island is only semi-tropical there is little weather variation between the seasons; it is warm and humid all year round but there tends to be a concentration of heavy rains and strong hurricane winds in the summer months. Because of this and the frequent occurrences of earthquakes, buildings had to be strong but flexible, with streamlined roofs and storm shutters, as well as carefully ventilated for those who had been used to the rather cooler climes of the British Isles.

The typical great house is a compact, double-pile structure built on the 'piano nobile' principle with an arcaded and often vaulted lower storey of stone for use as storage space. The living quarters, on the first floor, were usually built of timber, clad in butt-jointed boards (which can look remarkably like ashlar) and decorated with a lead-based paint sprinkled with fine sand to reflect the heat and repel the termite. For coolness, these first floor rooms were often left open to the roof, which was covered in native cedar shingles, pitched low, and hipped at the ends so as to reduce its exposure to high winds. The high rooflight windows commonly associated with these pitched shingled roofs also provided good cross-ventilation. The height of the front door, which was on this first floor, meant that access from ground level had to be by an external stairway. Verandahs, now almost universal on account of the coolness they offer and the extra covered space they provide, were almost certainly a relatively late addition to many of the early houses. Some of them show traces of Georgian detail, but are unlikely to date back much further than 1880.

In the construction of these great houses the availability of materials has also been an interesting contributing factor in producing adaptations of English and Scottish building traditions. To a certain extent it was possible to use the indigenous hardwoods of the island such as mahogany, mahoe, cedar and Spanish elm in both building and furniture. Perfectly cut squared stones were used for the construction of lower walls and wide flagstones for floors and steps as well as the occasional imported brick. Most of the ironwork would also have come to Jamaica as ballast on British ships. Evidently good building materials were exceedingly hard to come by: the restoration of Jamaican plantation houses usually reveals that many of the old timbers have old mortises in them, thus indicating that they had been used before.

There is little temporal continuity in the development of Jamaican architecture. Endless combinations and permutations of European building traditions evolved. The greatest force behind the perpetuation of such a variety was not the passing of time but rather the extraordinary eccentricity of some of the patrons who commissioned these plantation houses. Hampden Great House is a typical example of the architecture that these eccentric landowners inspired.

In 1787 the owners of Hampden Plantation invited their cousin, Philip Ainslie, out from Scotland for a visit. Ainslies had long been interested in the Caribbean. William Ainslie of Blackhill was a subscriber to the 'Company of Scotland' in 1696.[8] From Philip Ainslie's descriptions it appears Hampden was quite heavily fortified considering that life in Jamaica at this stage in the island's history was relatively stable:

> Very pleasing were my first impressions of Hampden, my cousin's Jamaica home. The residence of Mr Stirling, or, called in Jamaica parlance the great house, was of large dimensions, and built entirely of stone—a circumstance of rear (sic) occurrence in the country districts of Jamaica. The walls were very thick—a great advantage in so hot a climate, by adding to the coolness of the interior. The house contained a large hall running through its entire centre; to the right and left were other rooms, and further on, where a staircase ascends to an upper floor, were additional bedrooms.
>
> The windows were all glazed and on each side of them were loopholes

SOPHIE DRINKALL

for defence, which were also on each side of the entrance doors. Under
the hall were spacious cellars and the accommodation for men servants;
and as a further means for defence, there were loopholes or apertures, cut
in the floors of the hall and bedrooms, to allow a fire of musketry being
kept up against any assailants gaining possession of the cellars and rooms of
the ground floor of the house. The kitchen, as is always the case, was in
an adjoining building . . . Owing to there being several large ponds
around Hampden, it was considered far from healthy; and, as proof of this,
at a short distance infront of the great house appeared a tomb, the last
resting place of Patrick Stirling the eldest brother of my cousins, who
died after a short residence at Hampden.[9]

Perhaps the eccentric paranoia that inspired Mr Stirling's heavy fortifications was not
that misguided after all. In 1832 a series of rebellions by slaves destroyed a large number
of the island's beautiful estate buildings including much of 'Hamden do', as it is here
described. Ainslie, having been afforded his introduction to the island by his kinsmen,
went on to make a moderately successful colonial career for himself by taking up the
position of bookkeeper at Retirement Plantation.

On all the British Caribbean islands there are many examples of simple rectangular
houses with Early Georgian or Queen Anne details. James Gibbs was the main influence
behind this type of Jamaican great house. His style is simpler and more conservative than
those of his Palladian contemporaries, harking back to seventeenth century architects
such as Christopher Wren, John Webb, Roger Pratt and Hugh May. Through his *Book
of Architecture*, Gibbs had a greater influence on both provincial British and colonial
architecture in the eighteenth century than any other architect. Many of his designs were
published in his own book and a handful more in William Adam's *Vitruvius Scoticus*,
published in 1812. This latter book became particularly popular in the colonies since it
contained numerous designs for small scale buildings.

There is no better example in Jamaica of the 'Wren-style' house, as illustrated in
Gibb's book, than Annandale Great House (Fig. 4). William, Earl of Annandale, was
Lord President of the Parliament of Scotland in 1695 when the possibilities of a
'Company of Scotland' were still a burning issue.[10] The mid-eighteenth century plantation house that bears his name must have been viewed as an aesthetic triumph by those
later Scotsmen who managed to make a success of trading in the island where their
forbears, through no fault of their own, had suffered so much misfortune and ill-
treatment. The flat classical symmetry of this Jamaican house with its central fanlight
over the front door has an air of simple dignity.

Cardiff Hall, built in 1755, was the first building on the island of Gibbsian proportions
(Fig. 5). Cardiff Hall is the ideal example of the simple block plan, with the hall and
staircase on either side, which evolved into the central block with wings. Unlike
Annandale it does make one important concession to climate: it has a hurricane shelter

62)

4. Annandale Great House, built c.1760, an example of the type of classicism illustrated by James Gibbs in his small scale designs which were popular in Jamaica. (Institute of Jamaica)

5. Cardiff Hall, built in 1755, was the first plantation house in Jamaica to adhere to Gibbsian proportions. (Institute of Jamaica)

63)

6. Marlborough Great House, built c.1772, is one of the more Palladian inspired villas in Jamaica. It is believed to have been built by a Scottish master mason known to us only as 'Forsyte'. (Institute of Jamaica).

in the form of a vaulted chamber half dug out of the rock at the front of the main building. The Cardiff property was ceded to Daniel Blagrove by Cromwell for his part in the regicide of Charles I. He was, incidentally, the only man never to be called to justice for his involvement in the Stuart's death. All the buildings on the property—the slave hospital, the busha's house, the chapel and the unusual stone gate-houses, with pepperpot roofs—are of a similar style, fine design and are of the same high quality cutstone masonry work. If, as seems likely, they are of the same hand and the same master builder, believed to be a Scotsman, responsible for all the buildings, then a plaque set into the wall of the great house and engraved 'Forsyte', may in time help to identify him. He was, possibly, one of the many Forsyths who emigrated to the island.

'Forsyte' was probably the hand behind the construction of one of the more Palladian inspired villas in Jamaica. Marlborough Great House, built around 1772, is composed of a central block with wings (Fig. 6). Marlborough is constructed of stuccoed masonry on a stone basement, with a classical entrance portico, the pediment supported by solid mahogany pillars. A perron staircase leads up to the fanlighted entrance door. The hipped roof and chimney are hidden behind a high parapet and cornice. Inside a long hall runs from front to back where there is a Palladian window. There are rooms on either side of the hall, and a straight stair running down the back entrance to the garden. On either side of the front of the house is a low stone wall, connecting it with small office buildings of wood, which echo the main house in their quoined and pedimented facades with fanlighted doorways. Although relatively small, this is a perfect pattern-book house.

The deliberate Italianate Palladianism of the design of Marlborough Great House within this British colonial setting of Jamaica was not entirely altruistic. It cannot be explained simply in terms of aesthetical taste. J.S. Ackerman, in his *Palladio's Villas*, makes some interesting parallels between the use of this form of classicism and the state of the Veneto in the sixteenth century. With the decline of maritime trade in Venice, the Venetian aristocracy turned increasingly to farming and improving or reclaiming land in the Veneto between approximately 1510 and 1580. This emergence of a new type of country landowner who, for the first time in modern history, was economically tied to the land, coincided directly with the creation of Palladio's country villa form. As Ackerman points out, a classical education and the ambitions of a humanist gave this type of patron 'city tastes'.[11]

As it was for the Venetian aristocrat, so it was for the typical eighteenth century colonist. Although he probably stood outside the mainstream of British society, perhaps the younger and therefore impecunious son of a wealthy family, nevertheless he will have appreciated the authority and status that this architectural classicism afforded him.[12] At Marlborough, the Palladian leitmotif of a temple pediment and colonnaded porch provides the house with a great climactic central structure, that aesthetic command over the rest of the estate that Palladio deemed necessary according to his beliefs in both decorum and hierarchy:

> Io ho fatto in tutte le fabriche de Villa, e ancho in alcune della Città il Frontispicio nella facciata dinanti; nella quale sono le porte principali perchioche questi tali Frontispici accusano l'entrata della casa, e servono molto alla grandezza, e magnificenza dell'opera; facendosi in questo modo le parte dinanti più eminente dell'altre parti.

The deliberate choice of the words 'grandezza' and 'magnificenza' leaves little doubt as to Palladio's intention—to ennoble and classicise the villa as enhancement of the rustic exile of his clients, learned gentlemen.[13]

John Summerson, in the context of American colonial architecture, points out that the names of the architects and builders are lost to us because there were no architects in the modern sense. 'As in most provincial work of the time in England houses were designed by their leading craftsmen who proceeded on the basis of some existing model and the owners' verbal instructions'.[14] The same must certainly be true of a distant colony like Jamaica. The fact that the plantation owners were so varied in background and frequently outside the mainstream of society meant that their solutions to architectural problems were equally diverse. The forms the great houses took articulate the aims and aspirations of the patron: be he of humble origin, anxious to make his fortune in a colony where he had never intended to settle, the offspring of a nobleman or a successful nabob with pretensions to architectural scholarship and employing craftsmen like 'Forsyte' to steep them in the land-based classicism of the Palladians, however strangely conceived. Whatever their origins, Scottish immigrants to Jamaica contributed a very great deal to the rich and varied plantation architecture of the island.

NOTES

1. Rev. Bridges, *Annals of Jamaica*, 1826, Vol. I, note LII, p. 402.

2. Edward Long, *History of Jamaica*, 1774, Vol. I, p. 244.

3. F. Cundall, 'The Darien Venture', *Hispanic Notes and Monographs*, New York 1926, p. 102.

4. Long, *op. cit.*, Vol. II, p. 286.

5. qv., *Calendar of State Papers—West Indies*, Dundas Papers, 1695–1703.

6. Long, *op. cit.*, Vol. II, p. 287.

7. See Note 5.

D. McGibbon & T. Ross, *The Castellated and Domestic Architecture of Scotland*, 1892, Vol. II, p. 41 and p. 554. McGibbon and Ross also stress the correspondence between Craighall and Castle Stewart in Scotland. These links, therefore, between the Jamaican Stewart's Castle and Craighall in Fife are perhaps not so tenuous after all.

8. See Note 5.

9. Ray Fremmer, 'A Visitor to Hampden', *The Gleaner*, 1st April 1984.

10. See Note 5.

Annandale recalls the main block of Robert Hooke's Nether Lypiatt Manor in Gloucestershire, although it is longer and lower in order to resist strong winds.

11. See J.S. Ackerman, *Palladio's Villas*, New York, 1967, pp. 8–12. Ackerman pursues the line already explored by Michelangelo Muraro in his *Civiltà delle Ville Venete*, Venice, 1964.

12. John and Alexander Erskine were typical Jamaican planters falling into the Ackerman/Muraro Palladian landowner category. They were related to Lord Dun, David Erskine, for whom William Adam built the House of Dun, near Montrose, Forfarshire, Scotland. Jacob Aemelius Irving, grandson of the founder of that family in Jamaica, wrote of his late eighteenth century ancestors: 'Elizabeth Irving, daughter of the founder of that family in the island, married John Erskine, a gentleman of position who owned the fine estate of Lima in the parish of St James. Eventually his son, Alexander Erskine, late of Bryanston Square, London and Balhall, Forfarshire, Scotland . . .' (Ray Fremmer, 'The Legend of Lima Great House', *The Gleaner*, 17th June 1984.)

Little remains of Lima Great House today but a handful of high quality cut stone, a testament to the fact that the Erskines built there Jamaica home with a thought to the future.

13. Andrea Palladio, *I Quattro Libri dell'Architettura*, Venice 1570, II, xvi, p. 69.

14. See John Summerson, *Architecture in Britain 1530–1830*, 1953, 5th revised edition, 1969, Appendix.

BIBLIOGRAPHY

Aberdeen Art Gallery, *In Praise of James Gibbs Architect 1682–1754*, catalogue for 16th November–7th December 1974.

Acworth, Angus W., *Buildings of Architectural or Historic Interest in the British West Indies*, London, 1951.
    —*Treasure in the Caribbean; A First Study of Georgian Buildings in the British West Indies*, London, 1949.

Adam, William, *Vitruvius Scoticus*, Edinburgh, 1811.

Binney, Marcus and Blain, Douglas, 'Jamaica Revival', *Landscape*, September 1988.

Bridges, Rev. George William, *Annals of Jamaica*, 1826.

Calendar of State Papers-West Indies and Dundas, NLS.

Concannon, T.A.L., 'The Great Houses of Jamaica' in *Ian Flemming Introduces Jamaica*, edited by Morris Cargill, 1965.

Cundall, F., 'The Darien Venture', *Hispanic Notes and Monographs*, New York 1926.

Devine, T.M., 'An eighteenth century business elite: Glasgow-West India merchants c.1750–1815' *Scottish Historical Revue*, No. 57 (1978) pp. 40–67.

Donaldson's *Clan of the Camerons*.

Dunn, Richard, *Sugar & Slaves: The Rise of the Planter Class in the English West Indies, 1624–1713*, New York, 1973.

Fremmer, Ray, 'A Visitor to Hampden', *The Gleaner*, 1st April 1984.

Gibbs, James, *Rules for drawing several parts of architecture . . .*, 1732
    —*A Book of Architecture, Containing Designs of Buildings & Ornaments*, 1728.

Insch, G.P., *Scottish Colonial Schemes 1620–1686*, Glasgow 1922.

Keith, T., *Scottish Trade with the Plantations before 1707*, 1909.

Kent, William, *The Designs of Inigo Jones*, 1727.

Leslie, Charles, *A New History of Jamaica from the Earliest Accounts to the Taking of Portobello*, London 1740.

MacGibbon, D. and Ross, T., *The Castellated and Domesticated Architecture of Scotland*, 1892.

Masson, Georgina, 'Palladian Villas as Rural Centres', *The Architectural Review* CXVIII, No. 703, July 1955, pp 17–20.

McDougall, Robin, 'Hunting the Georgian in Jamaica', *Apollo*, October 1971, pp 262–9.

Nugent, Maria, *Lady Nugent's Journal of Her Residence in Jamaica from 1801–1805*, revised edition by Philip Wright, 1966 (Inst. of Jamaica), 1839.

Palladio, Andrea, *The Architecture in Four Books*, Isaac Ware's version for Lord

Burlington, 1738.

Park, Helen, 'A List of Architectural Books Available in America Before the Revolution', *Jnl. of the Society of Architectural Historians*, October 1961, Vol. 20, pp 115–30.

Sheridan, R.B., 'The wealth of Jamaica in the eighteenth century', *Sugar and Slavery: an Economic History of the British West Indies 1623–1775*, pp 295–6; 475–86.

Stewart, John, of Ardvorlich, *A History of the Clan of Cameron*, 1974.

Summerson, John, *Architecture in Britain 1530–1830*, 5th revision, 1970.

DMITRI SHVIDKOVSKY

Classical Edinburgh and Russian Town-Planning of the Late 18th and Early 19th Centuries: The Role of William Hastie (1755–1832)

Classical Edinburgh is of great interest to Russian historians of town-planning, not only on account of the originality of its form and conception, but also because of its resemblance to Russian cities of the same time. The career of the Scottish architect William Hastie deserves special investigation, since it was he who played the key role in the reconstruction of Russian towns in the neoclassical period.[1] Both as planner and architect he transformed townscapes throughout Imperial Russia in the early 19th century.

IN the late 19th and early 20th centuries the whole environment of Russia was changed. This was the most fruitful period of town-planning activity in the whole history of the huge country. The first land surveys were carried out, and all the boundaries of towns, estates, villages and forests were determined. A new road system was established. A new type of manor house with landscaped park was developed on British lines, and reproduced in thousands of residences for the gentry. And during the same period all the towns (about 500) were replanned according to the wishes of Catherine the Great and her grandson Alexander.[2]

For a quarter of a century, from 1808 to 1832, the architect responsible for this process was the William Hastie. Since the architectural side of the reform of the environment was so important, this Scotsman was one of the few people in Russian history who managed to change the external appearance of the whole country. As head of the Imperial town-planning service, Hastie is known to have been responsible for more than 100 towns on the banks of the Volga as well as in Siberia, Crimea and the Ukraine.

William Hastie came to St Petersburg from Edinburgh at the very time when classical town-planning was taking shape in Scotland. He was born in 1755, but we know nothing of his early life in Edinburgh.[3] In 1784, together with other Scottish craftsmen, he was invited to Russia by Charles Cameron, who was at that time architect to the Russian court.[4] The resemblance between Hastie's early works and those of Cameron suggests that he was probably Cameron's pupil and chief assistant. In January 1795 Hastie married a British girl, Margaret Bruce, in St Petersburg.[5] Soon afterwards, in July of the same year, he was appointed architect of the provinces of Ekaterinoslav and Crimea by Catherine the Great.[5] This meant that he was responsible for town-planning in the south of Russia, but in 1799 he was dismissed, together with all the assistants of the Governor of those provinces, Prince Platon Zoubov, whom the new Emperor, Paul II, hated.

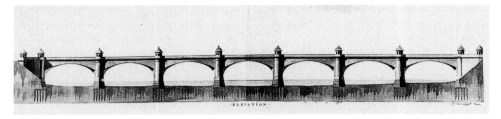

1. W. Hastie, design for a huge bridge over the River Neva, St Petersburg, one of a number of bridges he designed between 1806 and 1818. This scheme was never executed.

For the next two years Hastie was unable to find work in Russia, until Catherine's grandson, Alexander I, came to the throne in 1801, and the times of the great Empress came back, it seemed. The architect now began to work with James Wilson, a master smith from Edinburgh, who at that time was involved in the construction of a cast-iron factory near St Petersburg. This experience led Hastie to the designing of cast-iron bridges in the capital.[7] In 1805 the model for such a bridge was tested, and the first one was erected the next year. During the period 1806–18 he built the Krasny, Siny, Zhelty and Potseluev Bridges over the River Moika, and the Alexandrovsky Bridge over the canal in St Petersburg. He made designs for four further bridges over the Moyka, and suggested the construction of a huge one over the Neva, which was never fulfilled (Fig. 1).[8]

In 1808 he was engaged to carry out the construction of the new town of Tsarskoye Selo (Figs 2 and 3). This was a very important appointment. The town was to be built near the favourite imperial residence of the same name, and it was considered to be part of its ideal environment. The design made such a deep impression on the Emperor that it was not only put into effect, but the architect was created head of the country's town-planning service. The imperial decree said that Hastie 'is to be concerned with examining all the plans for provincial and district capitals'. In 1811 and 1812 the towns of Vyatka and Pokrov in Vyatka province, Spassk and Ardatov in Tambov province, Makar'ev in Nizhedorodskaya province, the capital of Saratov province and some towns of Kasan province were replanned.

The circumstances of the war with Napoleon brought Hastie a huge commission. Moscow was destroyed by fire during the stay of French troops in the old capital of Russia, with the loss of 6307 of the 9000 buildings in the city. In February 1813 Hastie was sent to make a plan for the reconstruction of the city, which he finished in July. Unfortunately Hastie's plan for Moscow has not survived, and we can only judge it on the basis of reconstructions, and the large number of written documents which have come down to us.[9] In his plan the city boundaries were simplified and made more regular. The most important point, for Hastie, was the creation of thoroughfares cutting through

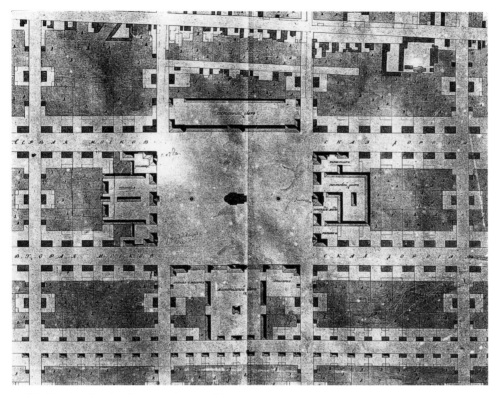

2. W. Hastie, plan for the central part of the new town of Tsarskoye Selo, 1809. This town plan, laid out near the royal palace of the same name, shows the impact of James Craig's plan for Edinburgh's first New Town.

3. W. Hastie, design for the buildings on the central square of Tsarskoye Selo, 1809. The clearly defined units and dignified symmetry suggest the impact of British Palladian and Georgian town-planning.

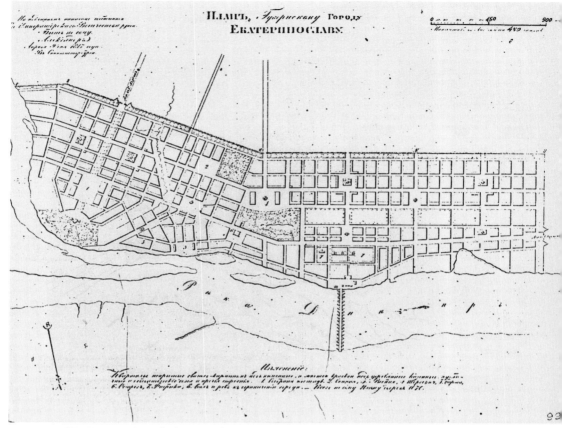

4. W. Hastie, plan of Ekaterinoslav, 1817. This ambitious plan, based on simple grid street patterns, was implemented under Hastie's personal direction.

the city from one end to the other. He tried to turn the main streets into wide, straight avenues and, in a number of cases, to create parallel thoroughfares in order to ease traffic movements.

Hastie devoted particular attention to the public spaces in Moscow. He supported the idea of concentric rings of wide boulevards on the site of the ancient fortress walls circling the city, in the Parisian manner. He also proposed considerably increasing the number of squares, creating new ones and straightening the outlines of the old ones. In his plan there were to be 47 squares altogether in Moscow, including 23 new ones. He also wanted to turn twelve of the existing large open spaces in the city, known as 'fields', into regularly designed parks.

Hastie's intention was to change the traditional planning and appearance of the ancient

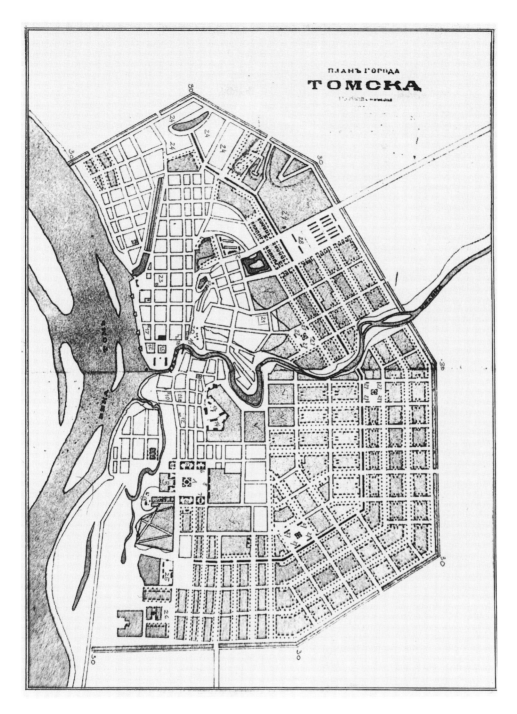

ПЛАНЪ ГОРОДА
ТОМСКА

5. W. Hastie, plan of Tomsk in Siberia, 1820. Here Hastie adapted his grid planning to fit into radial segments (with a result curiously reminiscent of the layout of Amsterdam, Ed.).

73)

6. W. Hastie, design of a model house, 1809. The influence of the Adam style is strongly evident.

Russian capital with amazing rapidity, within less than six months! Realising that it was not so simple, the Government had no money to put the scheme into effect.

Hastie returned to St Petersburg in the middle of 1813. In 1814 he worked on plans for Rodomysl', Skvira, Cherkas, Chirigin and Vasilikov–all towns in Kiev province. In 1815 he redesigned the plan of Smolensk and the nearby towns of Gzhatsk, Dykhovshchina and Krasnoy, and he drafted plans for Kiev.[10] In 1816 he worked on the planning of Vilno.[11] In all these cases he worked on the spot. His famous plan for Ekaterinoslav (now Dnepropetrovsk), which was carried out in full, was designed in 1817 (Fig. 4).[13] In the 1820s and 1830s he did a great deal of work on the Siberian towns of Omsk, Tomsk (Fig. 5) and Krasnoyarsk,[14] and on small towns in the Ukraine and the Volga region.[15] Most of these plans had been approved by the Emperor by 1829. This work continued until Hastie's death on 4 July 1832.

What new features were introduced into Russian town-planning during Hastie's time? Composition became more regular. A strictly rectilinear system began to predominate, in contrast to the radial, centralised structures composed of complex geometrical figures which had been popular under Catherine the Great. But the establishment of a firm, rigorous order was not at all. Hastie devised a system for regulating civic architecture at every level. Previously, during the second half of the 18th century, a more or less regular plan would have been formed, and the inhabitants could have chosen from among a small number of model designs (fewer than ten are known), although more often they built as they wished. Now, at the beginning of the 19th century, not only were regular plans

7. W. Hastie, design of a model house, 1809.

drawn up, but standard designs for all types of building were introduced. Moreover, their use was obligatory. Hastie alone made more than 50 designs for model houses (Figs. 6–8). An important point is that Hastie created a link between the standard house and the regular planning of the town: he developed a model system for laying out blocks in individual lots, and for arranging the houses in these blocks. He also designed model squares.

The designs for model houses, for private construction in the towns of the Russian Empire, were published in 1809, in a collection of facades containing projects by Hastie and the Italian Liugi Rusco, approved by His Imperial Majesty. In 1811 another album, also intended for obligatory use, was published; it contained 26 of Hastie's designs for blocks and squares. The sketches of the model houses show a large number of variants for the decoration of facades. There are very simple single-storey houses with three windows, and huge three-story mansions with wings at the sides. A great deal of inventiveness was required to combine unity of style with variety between the individual designs. His house designs were used in Smolensk, Saratov, Nizhniy Novgorod, Ufa, Staritsa, Kaluga and many other Russian towns.

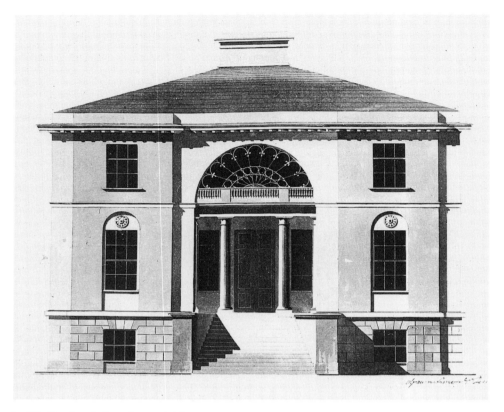

8. W. Hastie, design of a model house, 1809.

British ideas can also be detected in the designs for model blocks of houses. Many are particularly reminiscent of Edinburgh's first New Town, laid out to plans by James Craig from 1767 onwards, while individual houses recall Robert Adam's designs for small villas. In any case Hastie's town-planning method can be said to have developed to a large extent in parallel to that of his contemporaries in Britain. The less rectangular blocks recall the early 19th-century extensions to Edinburgh's New Town by Playfair and his contemporaries.

Hastie proposed constructing urban space of purely geometric forms. Irrespective of whether he was designing a residential quarter or a town square, he divided the areas into triangular, quadrilateral, circular, pentagonal or six-sided figures of every possible regular shape. As a result, any accidents of relief or of the old planning could be included in geometrically precise elements which fitted together like the pieces of a puzzle.

Another important point is that Hastie insisted in all cases that construction should be confined to the boundaries of the blocks, with regular shaped gardens placed in the centre, divided into equal-sized private plots. Thus, Hastie's town took on very definite

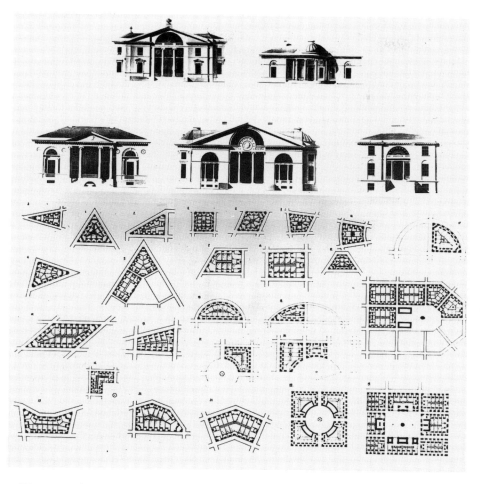

9. W. Hastie, designs of model houses, quarters and squares, showing block layouts arranged to fit sites of different shapes and sizes.

features (Fig. 9). Ideally it was a town with construction only around the perimeter of the blocks, with a regular distribution of blocks of similar size, a clear rhythm in the siting of the buildings, which were of similar size, and broad, geometrically shaped open spaces. Nature was subordinate to the pen and the decision of the architect. If we remember the model houses which the inhabitants were required by law to build—and also that other architects were working with or under Hastie, producing designs for shops, workshops and storehouses, as well as small farm buildings (barns &c), fences and gates—a complete picture of a regular, classical-style town comes into being. It was this ideal that Hastie strove to put into practice in his extensive town-planning work during the years 1810–30. Naturally, the reality of the old Russian towns brought changes to his plans, but Hastie tried to study these towns carefully, and he sometimes came into direct conflict with the local authorities and architects by insisting on changes.

We realise that Hastie was so insistent in his activity, because he had in his mind a clear town-planning ideal, which he had preserved from his Scottish youth.

Institute of History & Theory of Fine Arts,
Academy of Arts of the USSR, Moscow.

NOTES

1. H. Colvin, *A Biographical Dictionary of British Architects*. London, 1978, pp. 399–400; A. Cross, 'Cameron's Scottish workmen', *Scottish Slavonic Review*, Spring, 1988; A. Schmidt, 'William Hastie—Scottish planner of Russian towns', *Proceedings of the American Philosophical Society*, CXIV, 1970, pp. 226–243; M. Korshunova, 'W. Hastie in Russia', *Architectural History*, XVII, 1974.

2. T. Savarenskaya & D. Shvidkovsky, *Istoriya Gradostroitelnogo Iskusstva*, vol. II, Moscow, 1989, pp. 137–170.

3. Colvin, *op. cit.*, p. 399.

4. T. Talbot Rice, *Charles Cameron*, Edinburgh, 1967, p. 18; Cross, *op. cit.*, pp. 51–74.

5. Cross, *op. cit.*, p. 69.

6. CGIA (Central State Historical Archive of USSR), fond 1286, opus 2, n. 123, 1819, pp. 8–9.

7. CGIA, f. 1286, op. 2, n. 123, p. 10.

8. *Architecturnoye nasledstvo*, IV, 1953, pp. 210–211; 7, 1955, p. 143.

9. *Architecturnoye nasledstvo*, VIII, 1957, pp. 138–142.

10. CGIA, f. 1293, op. 166, n. 480(2), p. 1.

11. CGIA, f. 1286, op. 1, 1816, n. 6, pp. 1–33.

12. O. Shvidkovsky, *Dnepropetrovsk*, Moscow, 1954.

13. CGIA, f. 1293, op. 168, n. 17.

14. CGIA, f. 1286, op. 3, 1824, n. 313.

15. A. Osiatinsky, *Stroitelstvo gorodov na Volge*, Saratov, 1965, pp. 65–73.

William Henry Playfair's Design for a 'Roman Villa' at Lurgan in Northern Ireland

Playfair built two houses at Lurgan in Northern Ireland, Drumbanagher for Maxwell Close, and Brownlow House (later renamed Lurgan House) for his brother-in-law Charles Brownlow, later Baron Lurgan. This article identifies a splendid Greek-style preliminary scheme for Brownlow House, found in the Playfair drawings collections of the RIAS and Edinburgh University Library.

ALTHOUGH it is quite improper to suggest that Northern Ireland can be considered as 'abroad' it is nonetheless perhaps surprising that two of the finest houses by William Henry Playfair, the least travelled of architects, lay across the Irish sea. His career was dogged by ill health and, possibly, a tendency to hypochondria. Although best remembered today as a Greek Revival architect, he never showed any inclination to suffer the deprivations that necessarily accompanied the attempts of more robust architects to visit the purest source of ancient architecture. His visit to Italy came late in life and was motivated as much by a desire to obtain a second opinion from his brother, physician to the English colony in Florence, on the merits of the treatment advocated by his Edinburgh doctors.

As so often in his professional life, the Irish commissions arose from a very narrow circle of friendships. Following the death of his architect-father, Playfair, who had been born in London, was sent to Edinburgh so that his education could be supervised by his brilliant uncle, Professor John Playfair.

Like many of his University colleagues, the Professor, who was a bachelor, not only directly supervised the studies of his wealthier students, but offered them board and lodging in his house. Charles Brownlow, who inherited extensive Irish estates on the death of his father in 1822 was one of these pupils. In 1839 he was raised to the peerage as Baron Lurgan for services to the Whig party and this political persuasion may also have been imbibed at his Professor's fireside, for John Playfair had been a lifelong supporter of the party.

Playfair's first Irish commission, however, came not from Lord Lurgan himself but from his brother-in-law, Maxwell Close, who had married Anna Brownlow in 1820. The new house at Drumbanagher, although the locals seem to have known it as 'Close's Castle', was designed in 1829 and gave Playfair an opportunity to explore the Italianate style of Dunphail and Belmont, on the grandest possible scale. The house stood proudly on a ridge falling in terraces on the garden front. Playfair's exacting attention to every detail of its design ensured that it set an unusually high standard in Ireland and quality was controlled by the employment of tried and tested 'Edinburgh tradesmen'. Mrs Close took such an interest in the evolution of the design that Playfair dubbed her his 'Lady Patroness in architecture'.

The success of Drumbanagher brought out a degree of brotherly rivalry in Charles Brownlow who in, 1833, commissioned from Playfair a new house for Lurgan. Brownlow House (as the second house was known), was designed in the Elizabethan style, perhaps to be deliberately different from the architect's first Irish house. An additional spur to the new house, and a further incentive to the employment of Edinburgh craftsmen once again, must have been Charles Brownlow's second marriage in 1828 to Jane, the daughter of Roderick MacNeill of Barra.

Neither house has come down to us unscathed during Ireland's subsequent history. Drumbanagher has been demolished and its fine ashlar blocks were recycled in several local buildings. There was no chance of re-using the arched masonry of the porte cochère, of railway tunnel proportions, which still stands gauntly against the sky and defiantly towers over the more modest new house facing it across the drive. Brownlow is now occupied by the Orange Order and its interiors have been damaged in a fire-bomb attack. The exterior retains its astonishing silhouette and rears suddenly into view, like a stage set for a fairy tale, on the main Belfast-Dublin railway line.

Both houses could be entirely rebuilt from the complete sets of sequentially numbered office copies of the working drawings preserved in Edinburgh University Library, where they were sent by Playfair's trustees immediately following his death in 1857. Although no documentation appears to survive in Ireland for Drumbanagher, the estate accounts and an inventory for Brownlow are now in the Public Record Office in Northern Ireland although, sadly, there are no tradesmens' bills. Happily, the Record Office now also holds the working drawings for Brownlow including the full-size profiles which ensured the crispness of the final result.

The progress of both buildings can be gleaned from the two survivors of the set of annual letter books kept by the architect which are now also deposited in Edinburgh University Library. Further detail can to be found found in the rather more intimate letters from Playfair to his closest friends, the Rutherfurd family, in the National Library of Scotland.

Although Drumbanagher seems to have run fairly smoothly, with Playfair continuing to refine his design during construction, Charles Brownlow proved a maddeningly indecisive client. A number of designs were tried and found wanting until Playfair, after careful inspection of what he considered to be an exceptionally beautiful site, devised the dramatic design with its diagonal plan where the public rooms radiate like the spokes of the wheel to take advantage of the views but also recalls the Elizabethan's fascination with geometry.

The purpose of this article is not to examine the executed design for Brownlow in detail, but to publish the beautiful preliminary design for a Classical house with a noble

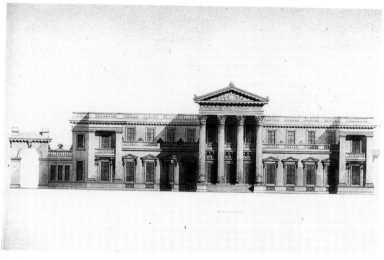

1. W.H. Playfair, unexecuted Classical style design for Brownlow House, Lurgan, 1833. Garden front. (Edinburgh University Library)

Corinthian portico, whose set of drawings is now split between the portfolios of Edinburgh University Library's Playfair Collection and the single Playfair portfolio of the Royal Incorporation of Architects in Scotland (Figs. 1–3). It is known that this design was 'in the style of a Roman villa' and that 'the first design was afterwards abandoned for an Elizabethan one'. The two sheets in the University's collection have been catalogued as 'Lurgan' although there are no inscriptions and this may therefore be a nineteenth century identification. The heraldic shield in the pediment appears to be only a sketch.

This would certainly fit this scheme with its great oversailing central temple-like portico and the clear volumes of its plan. As a design, in Irish terms, it would, if executed, have eclipsed the 'Grecian purity' of Wyatt's Castle Coole. Charles Brownlow, however was very concerned about the potential cost of his new house, and the grandeur of this portico possibly appeared prohibitive. Unquestionably the executed Elizabethan design was cheaper, as well as being considered more appropriate by Picturesque standards for its setting.

The copy letters reveal Playfair's mounting exasperation in trying to provoke Brownlow into taking a decision to build and the Closes were also appealed to in the hope of stimulating their brother into action. The executed design seems to have been built in two stages in an attempt to control costs, with the Dining Room added in the second phase when the original Lurgan House was recast to provide the offices. Even then Brownlow dragged his heels when it came to instructing the house-painter and Playfair's

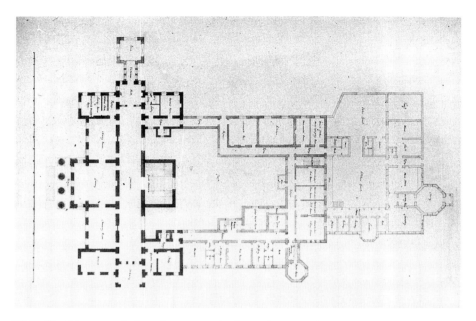

2. W.H. Playfair, ground plan of unexecuted scheme for Brownlow House, Lurgan. (Edinburgh University Library)

powers of diplomacy were severely tested before the room acquired his sumptuous colour scheme, planned so long before.

The final design gave general satisfaction as Playfair recorded in a letter to James Rutherford from the house in 1841:

> When you observe the date of this letter you will begin to think I have
> become a Wanderer on the face of the earth. I came over last Wednesday

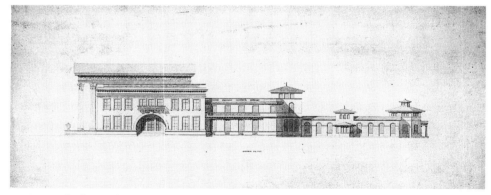

3. W.H. Playfair, side elevation of unexecuted scheme for Brownlow House, Lurgan. (RIAS Collection)

at the pressing request of Lord Lurgan which I was more inclined to obey, as I had not been here since the house was entirely finished and I was desirous of beholding my Elizabethan Child, Brownlow has had the Ground dressed up in the most admirable manner and my oriel windows stand out charmingly in the midst of smooth velvet turf, skilfully sprinkled with flowers and shrubs and surrounded by magnificent trees. In the hope that you will not think me conceited I may say that I think the House more comfortable and more like an old manor house than any modern attempt I have yet seen. In a few years when I expect to be dropping into the grave, I anticipate that it will possess the character of old age by weather stains and vegetable incrustations. Lord and Lady Lurgan are delighted with it and overwhelm me with kindness.

There are two remarkable things that have come to my knowledge since I was here, Lord Lurgan who is an active magistrate and well acquainted with the state of people tells me that it is quite unknown that an *unmarried* Woman should be got with child—And I observe that we go to bed every night in this luxurious house with all sorts of temptations to theft scattered about, and there is not a single shutter closed—so that any one might push up a sash and slip into any room from the lawn—so much for Irish Chastity and Irish Honesty.

The National Monuments Record of Scotland

ACKNOWLEDGEMENTS

The author would like to thank the present occupants of Drumbanagher and Brownlow, Hugh Dixon, and the staffs of the Public Record Office of Northern Ireland, the Special Collections Department of Edinburgh University Library, the Manuscripts Department of the National Libraries of Scotland and the Irish Architectural Archive.

NOTE of W.H. Playfair's Edinburgh Tradesmen employed at Brownlow House at Lurgan.

Payments 1838–1842. Builder: Charles MacGibbon £30,450; Plasterer: James Anderson £1,245 17s 8d; Plumber: John Allan £2,218 17s 10d; Interior decoration: D.R. Hay and Co. £2,236; Furniture and upholstery: Heirs of William Trotter £3,289 2s 7d.

(Public Record Office of Northern Ireland D1928/W/5.)

Areas of Hay's marbled wall faces, with fictive marble busts inset over the doors, survive in the Saloon as does a gilt 'Louis' style chimneyglass similar to Trotter work elsewhere. An 1848 Inventory by Dowell of George Street, Edinburgh acting for Jane, Lady Lurgan and Robert Pasley of Dublin acting for the young Lord Brownlow is also in the collection and confirms Playfair's report of the sumptuousness of the house.

ANNA VON AJKAY

James Souttar in Sweden

James Souttar (1840–1921), from Aberdeen, spent just over three years in Sweden, from 1863 to 1866. His work included the superintendence and the erection of the Church of Saint Peter and Sigfrid in Stockholm, more commonly known as 'The English Church'. He also made drawings for various projects in the capital and the country, which were not, however, realised. It is evident that he had an ambition to make the best possible use of the time for which he was contracted for the building of the church. Souttar's stay in Sweden can therefore be seen as sound professional training prior to his career in Aberdeen after his return in 1866.

AFTER an eight-year apprenticeship at Mackenzie and Matthews in Aberdeen 1852–60, James Souttar worked as a draftsman for Sir Matthew Digby Wyatt in London. After this he went on a tour to Belgium, France, Switzerland, Austria and Denmark.[1] We do not know how he became acquainted with Johan August Westerberg, a young architect in Gothenburg who was later highly productive, but Souttar was invited to stay with the hospitable Westerbergs in 1863. The father, who was a wholesaler and ship-owner, had commercial relations in Britain and the son, Johan August, had studied architecture in Germany, England and Scotland.[2] Gothenburg, which had the greatest export port in Sweden, was progressing with industrial growth in the 1850s and '60s. Souttar must have been stimulated by the British influence on cultural and social life and also by the new town-plan for the extended city, released in 1862, with its boulevard and a zone of parks.[3] He may have been interested in his friend's first large commission, the Church of Saint John (St Johanneskyrkan) in Gothenburg.[4] Friendship with the family led the following year to the marriage between Souttar and Johan August's younger sister, Maria Sophie Georgina. During the same year Westerberg wed Jemima Marshall Anderson from Aberdeen.

The English congregation in Stockholm had been worshipping for decades in hired meeting places. When in 1855 a chaplaincy was established, the chapel fund progressed and in 1861 a ground plot was acquired on Rörstrandsgatan in the northern part of the city. The site was far from attractive, having a prison and several highrise buildings next to it, but it was close to the most fashionable shopping street, Drottninggatan (Fig. 1). The church to be was financed by private subscriptions and a grant from H.M.'s Government.[5] The erection was somewhat adventurous with regard to having to adapt a scheme, acquired from an architect abroad, Gustavus W. Hamilton in Liverpool, to

1. The English Episcopal Church of Saint Peter and Sigfrid at Rörstrandsgatan in Stockholm, built 1864–65. The church was carefully demolished 1913 and rebuilt the same year in the residential area of foreign embassies on Strandvägen. (Photo City Museum, Stockholm, about 1900)

Swedish building regulations.[6] The drawings did not match the requirements and therefore were refused by the town architect of the housing authority in January 1863. Despite this the foundation was laid early in April–so early in the spring that the frost could hardly have left the ground. In July the construction could start with completed (unsigned) drawings which were approved of by the department of public works and the King in Council (Fig. 2).[7] In the following year half of the building was erected, but the walls started to subside owing to defective masonry and insufficient foundations. Now the churchbuilding committee decided to contract a new builder–the first one had committed suicide–and wisely also to appoint an architect. James Souttar, who applied in 1864, was given the commission to superintend the works.[8] He had in fact to start anew, right from the foundations. Living close to the building site[9] and assisted by a young Swedish draughtsman, A.E. Melander, he completed it 1865 and the following year the church was consecrated (Figs. 3 and 4).

It was quite a small church of Early Gothic design, built of red sandstone rough hewn,

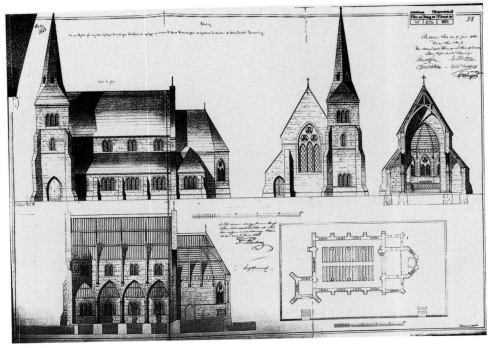

2. Unsigned drawings for the English Church, made in Stockholm from a scheme by Gustavus W. Hamilton in Liverpool. Approval by the King in Council above to the right 1863. A tower set on the side with entrance to the church was new in Sweden at this time. (Photo City Museum, Stockholm)

with apse and tower set on the side (Fig. 5). Inside the light stone walls were unplastered, mentioned as causing a sensation in an article. The aisles were mere passages but the nave with its finely proportioned arches seemed to be spacious, due to the high timber vaulting. The pavement was tiled in white (Fig. 6).[10] In 1913 the church was demolished and rebuilt in the residential area of embassies on Strandvägen by A.E. Melander, the former assistant of Souttar's.

Stockholm had a population of over 126,000 in 1865. During the 1860s technical conditions improved: water mains were laid, streets were repaved, quays were cobbled and gaslighting was introduced. Industrialisation was aided by the establishment of banking.[11] In 1863, when Stockholm got local autonomy, the authorities started to prepare a 'complete and definite plan for the future', including the expansion of the city to its rural boundaries.[12] The building of schools and hospitals was entrusted to élite architects.

Souttar received no commissions. Instead, he kept himself occupied by writing an illustrated article on 'A short account of the origin and development of Gothic Architec-

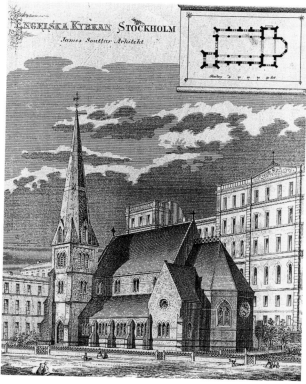

3. Plan and façade of the English Church, designs made by James Souttar to illustrate article in *Tidskrift för Byggnadskonst och Ingenjörsvetenskap*, 1864. (Photo City Museum, Stockholm)

ture in Britain' ('Kort beskrivning öfver ursprunget och utvecklingen af Götiska arkitekturen i England'). The essay, in Swedish, was published in the periodical *Tidskrift för Byggnadskonst och Ingenjörsvetenskap* (Journal of Architecture and Engineering Sciences) in 1866. The journal aimed to provide information about domestic and western building activities. Souttar kept abreast of current building plans; he made drawings and sent them to building proprietors.[13]

The Freemasons' orphanage on the outskirts of the town was a typical project. He designed two buildings, one for girls and one for boys, in the form of detached wings to the mansion of Kristineberg which belonged to the order (Figs. 7 and 8). One wing ended in a chapel with Early Gothic tracery in the windows. He intended using warm air circulation for heating instead of the usual glazed tile stoves. The commission, however, went to J.F. Åbom, the leading architect of the period.[14]

Souttar's entry for the competition for the town-planning of Karlstad on Lake Vänern is also of interest. The competition was announced some days after the great fire which

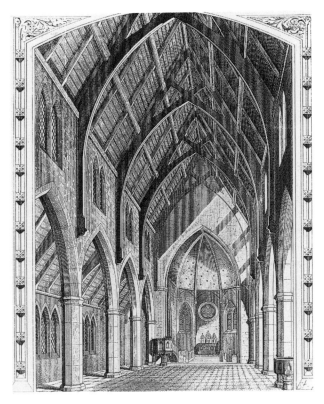

4. Interior. Pointed arched braces support the roof.

had devastated the dense wooden housing area in July 1865. Souttar concentrated first and foremost on the requirements for fire prevention and order: broad streets, large blocks and spacious ground plots (Fig. 9). However he did not give thought to the port and the future railway station. Souttar had also ignored the large market place which had been the focus of public, social and commercial life in every Swedish city since the Middle Ages. Instead, he designed a park surrounded by public buildings. It is clear that he proposed to transpose the English square into Karlstad. Neither his nor the other nineteen entries were accepted. The rebuilding of Karlstad was realised, as is often the case in similar circumstances, along the lines proposed by the planning committee itself.[15]

James Souttar was 23 years old when he came to Sweden. In Stockholm, where he spent just over three years, building activities were rather slow. His sole work, the English church, was somewhat out of the way, little known and not frequented by Swedes. Thus the building of the church did not give him the reputation which would have enabled him to compete with Swedish architects. Those who were commissioned

5. A close look on the English Church reveals the walls and the spire in coursed rubble of sandstone. The construction wholly in stone was a breathtaking novelty at this time. (Photo City Museum, Stockholm, about 1900)

were known through their education at the (Swedish) Royal Academy of Art. This was especially important with respect to State commissions for public buildings when drawings were scrutinised by the highest authority of public works. Souttar's colleague and brother-in-law, J.A. Westerberg, was young and at the start of his career, far away in Gothenburg. Still, Souttar gained from his experience in Sweden; the stay provided him with wide knowledge of the profession in his later career.

City Museum of Stockholm

NOTES
1. A.v. Ajkay, 'A.E. Melander', *Stenstadens arkitekter*, Stockholm 1981, pp. 81, 99.
2. J.A. Westerberg, *Svenskt Konstnärslexikon*, 1967, p. 638.

6. Interior of the English Church photographed about 1900. The church could seat 120 persons. In both aisles you can see the heating apparatus. (Photo City Museum, Stockholm)

3. *Tidskrift för Byggnadskonst och Ingenjörsvetenskap*, 'Om Göteborgs stads utvidgning', 1865, p. 38.

4. O. Nylén, *Från Börsen till Park Avenue 1850–1985*, Göteborg, 1988.

5. Rev. J. Howard Swinstead, *The English Church in Stockholm*, Stockholm, 1913, pp. 15–20.

6. The English Church Archives, A III:2a.

7. Byggnadsnämndens arkiv, Lindbacken 4(24) 1863:36–38, City Archives, Stockholm.

8. The English Church Archives A III:2a.

9. Mantalslängd Klara Nedre, 1865:4011, 1866:4129, City Archives Souttar lived in a flat with his wife on Barnhusträdgårdsgatan 15. Their first child, Gina, was born there in 1865.

10. The article 'Engelska kyrkan i Stockholm', *Tidskrift för Byggnadskonst och Ingenjörsvetenskap* 1864, pp. 156–58. Illustrations were made by James Souttar.

11. K. Mandén-Örn, '1850–70', *Husen på Malmarna*, Stockholm 1985, pp. 63–80.

12. M. Råberg, 'The development of Stockholm since the Seventeenth Century', *Growth and Transformation of the Modern City*, Stockholm, 1979.

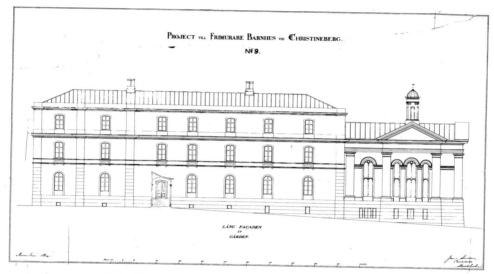

7. Garden façade of the Freemasons' orphanage in Kristineberg by James Souttar, 1864. The sparse window-setting was typical for the period. The commission however was given to the élite architect J.F. Åbom. (Photo City Archives, Stockholm)

8. Second floor of the Freemasons' orphanage. Left: girls department, right: boys department with sleeping quarters. Note that only the girls have a large clothes store. Souttar placed the diningroom, dayroom, kitchen and bathroom on the ground floor. (Photo City Archives, Stockholm)

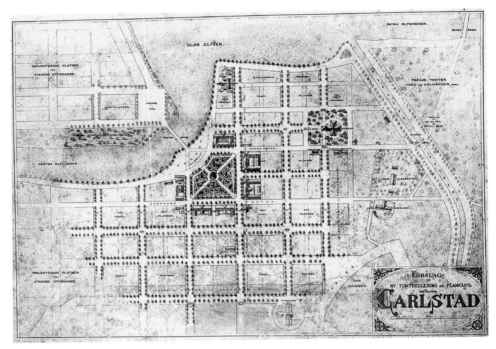

9. Town-plan for the city of Karlstad by James Souttar, 1865. Note the tree-lined broad streets. The park-square instead of an open market place was completely unknown in Swedish towns. The town-plan was not accepted. (City engineer's office in Karlstad. Photo: Professor Göran Lindahl, 1965)

13. E. Hultmark, *Kungl. Akademien för de fria konsterna utställningar 1794– 1884*, Stockholm 1935, p. 486.
14. Nya ritningssamlingen NS 9:4, 6, 8, City Archives, Stockholm.
15. G. Lindahl, 'Karlstad 1865, Stadsbyggande för 100 år sedan', *Värmland Förr och Nu*, 1965, pp. 12–73.

Scottish Architects in the Far East: 1840–1870

Among the foreign architects and civil engineers active in the Far East between 1860 and 1940 were a number of Scotsmen. One of the most successful was the Victorian architect William Kidner, but records of his interventions at RIBA meetings show that he acquired only limited knowledge of traditional Chinese and Japanese architecture in the course of his practice abroad.

THE Institute of Asian Architecture[1] began compiling a list of existing architectural treasures in major Asian cities in October 1987, when it was first granted research assistance by the Toyota Foundation. Except for Japanese cities, which had been covered previously, during the first three years 17 cities in China, Korea, Taiwan, Hong Kong and Macau were covered by the collaboration of a group of international researchers, and the results will be published soon.

Through this research, it was realised that almost all the buildings standing in these cities were constructed by foreign powers and capitalists from 1860–1940. As the British then played a leading world role in politics and economics, the majority of the architects and civil engineers in the Far East were from Britain, mostly from Scotland. Their names and occupations are recorded in contemporary documents such as newspapers, consular gazettes, directories, and public records. It is, however very difficult to know why they set sail for the Far East. They must have been looking for better paid, or more challenging, jobs and probably had personal connections in the Far East.

From 1840 to 1870, it was mainly royal engineers and civil engineers who were responsible for construction works in the British colonies and settlements, and so only two Western architects were present in Hong Kong in the mid-1840s. But little is known of their work or personal connections. Edward Ashworth,[2] of Exeter, and George Strauchan,[3] of Edinburgh, both worked at Hong Kong around 1845, and the two designed almost all the early merchants' buildings there. The latter is known to have designed the Hong Kong Club (1845) and the George Burnet Company's office in Shanghai (1851), and to have worked in Shanghai until he left China in 1854. According to William Kingsmill (1837–1910),[4] the first President of the Society of Engineers and Architects in China,[5] Strauchan preferred the Greek Revival style, with two-storied colonnades, or verandahs in Asian terminology, probably because the style was thought to suit tropical and subtropical zones. He designed buildings in that style, which adorned the Bund of Shanghai and the Praya of Hong Kong during the 1840s and 50s. But they were soon

1. William Kidner, Hong Kong and Shanghai Bank at Shanghai, China, 1877. Despite the Chinese figures in the street, this is an ostentatiously European, classical style building. (Illustration from *The Architect*, 6 October 1877)

destroyed by heavy rain, humidity and typhoons. Thus, unfortunately, few buildings of this period remain.

The foreign architects of the next 20 years are represented by William Kidner (1841–1900). Nothing about his early career is known, except that he first came to China in 1866 to supervise the construction of the Holy Trinity Cathedral in Shanghai.[6] The original design had been drawn by G.G. Scott, who was often commissioned to provide designs for Anglican churches abroad. There were certain connections between the two, but G.G. Scott's biography and even his nomination papers for Fellow of the R.I.B.A. reveal nothing. Since the foreign community in Shanghai had been eager for a new style of architecture and a qualified architect, Kidner was commissioned to design commercial buildings, as well as a Gothic church in Hankow (1867)[7] and a prison for the Shanghai British Consulate (1867).[8] It is thought that he settled down in Shanghai for some time after the completion of the cathedral in 1869.

Unlike G.G. Scott, Kidner himself was not a Gothicist, and changed architectural style upon demand. The Hong Kong and Shanghai Bank (1877)[9] (Fig. 1) and the Mercantile Bank (1878) were his major works in Shanghai. They were so richly adorned

2. William Kidner, Church for the British North Borneo Company's Settlement, Kudat, 1885. Here Kidner shows a greater sensitivity to local (here tropical) climatic conditions, but only limited awareness of the region's traditional architecture. (Illustration from *The Builder*, 11 July 1885)

with elaborate Neo-Classical motifs that it must had been enough to surprise any Chinese. Although he was the only architect in Shanghai during the 1860s and must had been asked to design buildings by many Europeans, he was actually not very prolific, and only a few buildings in Shanghai have been identified as his work. Returning home in 1878, he designed some country houses in Elgin in his own style, 'grasping any motif of any origin so long as it contributes to the fun'.[10] After working for some years, he once again sailed for the Far East in 1885 to design a church[11] (Fig. 2) and a government house[12] for the British North Borneo Company, which had been established in 1881 by Rutherford Alcock, former British Minister to China. They no doubt had known each other since their stays in China. The government house he designed for the North Borneo Company has an ordinary plan suited to a tropical monsoon climate, with spacious rooms and wide verandahs around them and framed with rigid pillars, while the style is very curious, with Hindo-Islamic arches in the porte-cochère, curved cantilevers supporting deep eaves and a gabled roof, all devised to refer to Malay culture. He was the first to adapt local architectural tradition to British Imperial buildings in the Far East, although William Emerson had been doing so in India since the 1870s.

While practising in Shanghai, Kidner visited various places in China and Japan. Although some leading British architects were eager to know of Far Eastern architecture, he never reported on it. He visited in and around Yokohama, probably for sight-seeing or summering because Nagasaki and Yokohama had come to be regarded by the foreign community in Shanghai as the healthiest places among the treaty ports open in China and Japan. Then, when Joshia Conder (1850–1921), F.R.I.B.A., professor of architecture at the Japanese Imperial College of Engineering from 1877 to 1884, presented his first paper on Japanese architecture[13] to the R.I.B.A., read at the general meeting in March 1878 by T. Roger Smith, J. Conder's previous teacher, Kidner testified 'to the extreme accuracy of the descriptions' and answered questions by members on the author's behalf. Compared with Conder's accuracy, Kidner's answers seem to have missed the point. For example, he should have answered 'Shinto-shrine gate (*Torii*)' instead of 'monument of erected to virtuous widows', when asked to explain 'the meaning of the symbol on the tomb or monument of double trabeated form which appeared in nearly all the photographs exhibited'.[14] Kidner shared the prejudice against Far Eastern architecture that 'there was no architecture, as we in Western Europe understood the word' with his contemporaries, such as J. Fergusson, T.R. Smith and P. Spiers.

The name of Kidner once again appeared in the R.I.B.A. General Meeting of 19 November, 1894, at which he read a paper entitled 'Notes upon the Architecture of China' prepared by Frederick M. Gratton (??–1918), F.R.I.B.A., Shanghai.[15] Since Gratton had been in China since 1881, Kidner must have visited China to become acquainted with him, probably while designing some buildings for the North Borneo Company. From an Asian view point, Gratton's papers seem to be preferable as he first recognized the existence of Chinese architecture and correctly evaluated the national style of architecture. Reading the papers, Kidner was asked nothing about Chinese architecture, except one question by W. Emerson about the materials of the large statues of Buddha, to which he replied 'these were made of plaster', comparing them with a large Japanese statue of Buddha in Kamakura, outside Yokohama.[16] It is clear that Kidner was regarded in Britain as one familiar with Far Eastern architecture as late as the 1890s, although his knowledge was actually too little to allow him accurately to introduce Conder's and Gratton's papers to the British. Kidner was merely an architect unrestricted to any particular architectural style or region, not an architectural historian.

The Scottish connection is more apparent in civil engineering than in architecture. Robert Henry Brunton (1841–1901), M.I.C.E., of Aberdeenshire, was the first British engineer hired by the Japanese Government.[17] Recommended by Stevenson Brother of the Scottish Lighthouse Board, he was appointed as chief engineer in the Japanese Department of Lighthouses in 1868, and arrived in Yokohama with two assistants, Colin

A. McVean and A.W. Blundell. Since the Japanese government then had only one department related to public works, Brunton, as the one qualified civil engineer, was necessarily asked for advice by the Japanese government, which was about to set up the Ministry of Public Works. In 1870, he recommended MacVean as chief surveyor for the Department of Survey. McVean soon started ordnance surveys all over Japan, and provided plans for some of the buildings of the Imperial College of Engineering, now the Faculty of Engineering, University of Tokyo.[18] He ordered a quantity of fittings and building materials for the buildings from Glasgow through his friend, Campbell Douglas, Glasgow, and asked him to recommend 'a good architectural draftsman, of quick and skilful resources'.[19]

Douglas recommended the Frenchman, Charles Alfred Castel de Boinville (1850–1897), who had been articled first under William Henry White, future secretary of R.I.B.A., and then under Douglas. As soon as he arrived in Japan in 1872, de Boinville showed considerable ability as an architect and was commissioned, instead of MacVean, to design many important buildings for the Japanese government, such as the remaining buildings of the Imperial College of Engineering, the Akasaka Imperial Guest House and Banqueting Hall, and the building of the Ministry of Foreign Affairs. During his stay in Japan, de Boinville never became interested in Japanese architecture, in contrast to Conder. Retiring from the Japanese Ministry of Public Works in 1882, de Boinville entered the Office of Works as an architect, and then was appointed as Surveyor of the India Office.

Brunton, on the other hand, played an important role in the development of modern technology in Japan, and was greatly appreciated by the Japanese. The Japanese Institute of Civil Engineering, the Department of Lighthouses and the Yokohama City Office will jointly celebrate the 150th anniversary of Brunton's birth this year.

> *Institute of Art and Design,*
> *University of Tsukuba, Japan.*

NOTES

1. Professor Fujimori Terunobu, University of Tokyo, is the representative for this scheme.

2. E. Ashworth, 'How Chinese Workers Built an English House', *Builder*, 1 Nov. 1851, pp. 686–8.

3. E.J. Eitel, *Europe in China*, 1895, p. 248.

4. W. Kingsmill, 'Early architecture in Shanghai', *North China Herald*, 24 November 1893.

5. Established in 1901 in Shanghai.

6. G.G. Scott, *Personal and Professional Recollections*, 1879.

7. His drawing is preserved in the Maps and Drawings Collection of the Public Record Office, Kew.

8. FO17/1303, Letter of Edmund Hornby, Chief Judge to Lord Stanley, dated 5 August 1867.

9. Illustration in *Architect*, 6 October 1877, description p. 185.

10. C. McKean, *Moray: an Illustrated Architectural Guide*, 1987, pp. 41–43.

11. 'Illustration of Church of the British North Borneo Company's Settlement, Kudat', *Builder*, 11 July 1885.

12. 'Illustration of Government House, Sandakan', *Builder*, 5 December 1885.

13. J. Conder, 'Notes on Japanese Architecture', *R.I.B.A. Transactions*, 1878–79.

14. Discussion papers were introduced in 'The Architecture of Japan', *Builder*, 13 April 1878, pp. 386–7.

15. *R.I.B.A. Transactions*, 1894.

16. 'The Architecture of China', *Builder*, 24 November 1894, pp. 371–2.

17. Obituary, *M.I.C.E. Proceedings*, 1900–01.

18. Letter of Vice Consul Dohmen to Mr. Adams, 15 February 1872, *British Parliamentary Papers*.

19. *R.I.B.A. Journal*, 1897.

Design Inspiration from Abroad: A Review of Three Continental Sketchbooks

THE books of architectural drawings compiled by Scottish archi-
tects in the aftermath of their continental sketching tours in the years around 1900
constitute invaluable reference material and provide a veritable feast for the eye. They
offer a rich pool of information on the authors, notably their preferences and sources of
inspiration.[1] By default, some works are better known than others, and three in
particular deserve greater attention: William J. Anderson's *Architectural Studies in Italy*
(1890), Andrew Noble Prentice's *Renaissance Architecture and Ornament in Spain* (1894) and
James A. Arnott and John Wilson's *The Petit Trianon* (three volumes, 1907, 1908).[2] The
following review shows that these texts deserve to be better known.

Each of the large volumes was issued as a limited edition, beautifully presented. Those
by Prentice and Anderson include illuminating lists of subscribers, indicating the range
of their contacts even at an early stage in their careers. The success of the volumes may
be measured by their use as reference sources for the various editions of *The History of
Architecture* by Professor Banister Fletcher and his son, who graciously acknowledge the
texts. This kind of recognition served as publicity for the authors, an advantage they will
have perceived before considering publication. The monographs illustrated their
academic calibre and skills of draughtsmanship to impress potential clients.

All four authors succeed in conveying an infectious enthusiasm for their subject and
for the benefits derived from such a form of study. Anderson, for example, praises the
refinements of proportion, careful massing, the appropriate subordination and harmony
of details in 'the perfected period of the whole classical revival', the early sixteenth
century in Italy, while Prentice expresses surprise that the beautiful masterpieces of the
Plateresque period in Spain should be so little known, and Arnott and Wilson celebrate
the Petit Trianon as 'a complete example of French architecture of the best period of
the eighteenth century'.[3] The design inspiration gained from sketching at first hand,
measuring and analysing an historic building and its details, was duly recognised by
the authors who were eager to share their findings, tangible and intangible, with their
professional colleagues. Sketching was established as part of an architect's elementary
training by the late nineteenth century. The educational potential of the publications was
perceived most particularly by Anderson, who demonstrated a clear-sightedness appropriate to the future Director of the Department of Architecture at Glasgow School of
Art in subtitling his work 'A General View for the Use of Students and Others'.
However, they were not intended, to serve as pattern books providing 'models for

imitation', as Anderson stressed; they were either aimed at those seeking inspiration with the style in hand, or else were to be enjoyed purely for their inherent interest.

The reader of each publication is specifically asked by the author to note that the sketches were made and measured on the spot (with one or two named exceptions), demonstrating that they deemed it necessary to verify the accuracy of the drawings. Similarly, each author pre-empts any queries regarding the seemingly random order of the plates by explaining that they follow the sequence of their route, or method of progress.

Anderson's *Architectural Studies in Italy* is the earliest of the three publications under review; he was the first winner of the Alexander Thomson Scholarship in 1887 and dedicated his work to the Trustees.[4] It contains an inspirational array of plates, several illustrating the works of Baldassare Peruzzi (1481–1536), whom Anderson held in high regard. The format and choice of subjects echo the earlier folio by John Kinross, *Details from Italian Buildings Chiefly Renaissance*, a copy of which was held by the Glasgow Architectural Association with which Anderson was actively involved.

The text accompanying the plate of Como Cathedral, an early Renaissance masterpiece by Tommaso Rodario, is typical of the concise and informative notes to the drawings: in it he analyses what is important about the building and gives the reader a sense of scale by detailing the measurements of the buttresses on the apsidal transept and aisle (Fig. 1). Exterior elevations may be instructive for their overall composition and proportions but Anderson was equally struck by their components, the portals, the *campanili*, and details such as pilasters. The illustration of the marble pulpit from Sant Annunziata, Genoa, is explained helpfully: since it is sited in a richly decorated church it is no surprise to learn that the red and white marble is inlaid with a colourful array of expensive stones (Fig. 2). Turning to the form of the structure he notes the unusual absence of an entablature between pier and arch but praises the simple, yet grand effect which results. This freedom of design in Renaissance architecture, so admired by Anderson, was translated into his own work, in the free composition of Orient House, McPhater Street, Glasgow, 1892, for example, a landmark in his regrettably curtailed career.

While the Italian Renaissance had been the subject of many publications, Andrew Prentice perceived a fresh, untapped source of Renaissance design inspiration in the early sixteenth century architecture of Spain, first studied by him on his travels as the Soane Medallist in 1888.[5] He was struck by the transitional nature of the Plateresque work, Gothic applied with Renaissance detailing, giving a fusion of Romanesque strength and reserve and Moorish beauty and delicacy. He served his apprenticeship with William Leiper and will almost certainly have crossed paths in this office with William Anderson, then working as draughtsman: the decision to publish his studies may have been instigated by the latter's example and persuasion.

1. Architectural Studies in Italy, plate xL. South aisle wall and apsidal transept of Como Cathedral.

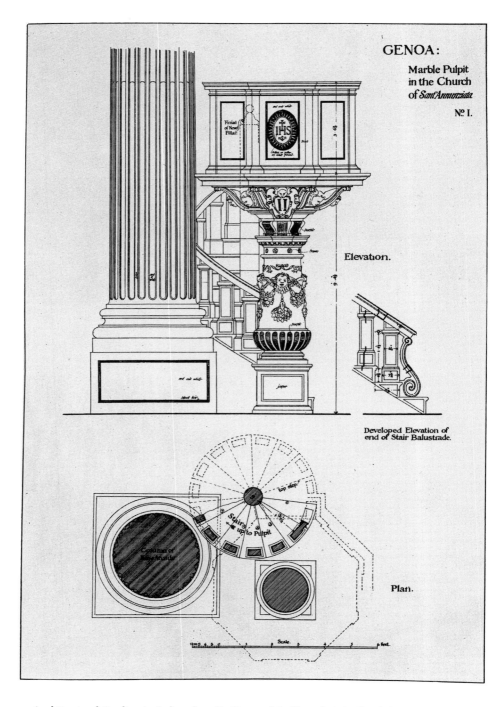

GENOA:

Marble Pulpit
in the Church
of *Sant'Annunziata*

Nº I.

Elevation.

Developed Elevation of
end of Stair Balustrade.

Plan.

Scale.

2. Architectural Studies in Italy, plate II. Genoa. Marble pulpit in Sant' Annunziata.

Within the drawing:

ALCALA DE HENARES
Detail of windows
from the façade
of the University

Section.

Scale of feet &c.

Stone Seat

Ground line

3. Renaissance Architecture and Ornament in Spain, plate 32. Alcala de Henares. Detail of window from facade of university.

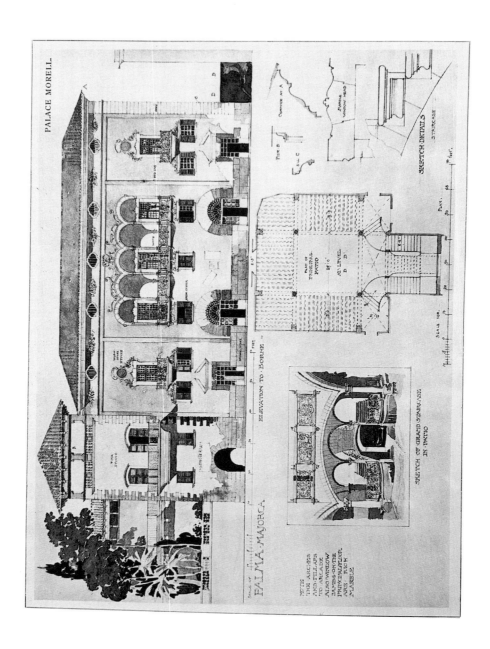

4. Renaissance Architecture and Ornament in Spain, plate 56. Palace Morell, Palma Majorca.

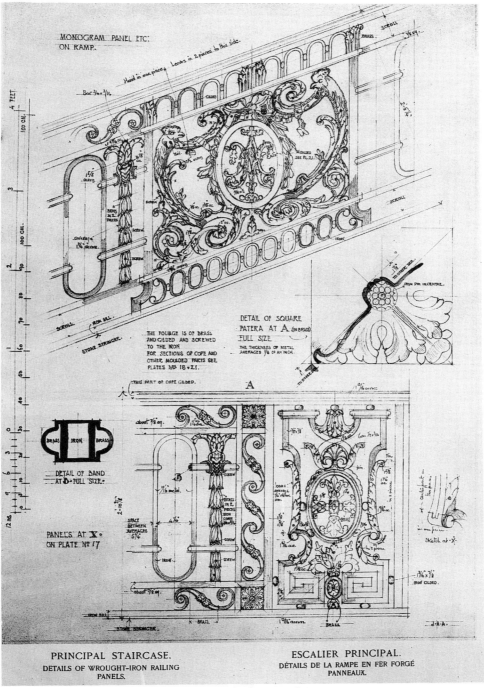

PRINCIPAL STAIRCASE.
DETAILS OF WROUGHT-IRON RAILING
PANELS.

ESCALIER PRINCIPAL.
DÉTAILS DE LA RAMPE EN FER FORGÉ
PANNEAUX.

5. The Petit Trianon, vol III, plate xix. Detail of Principal Staircase.

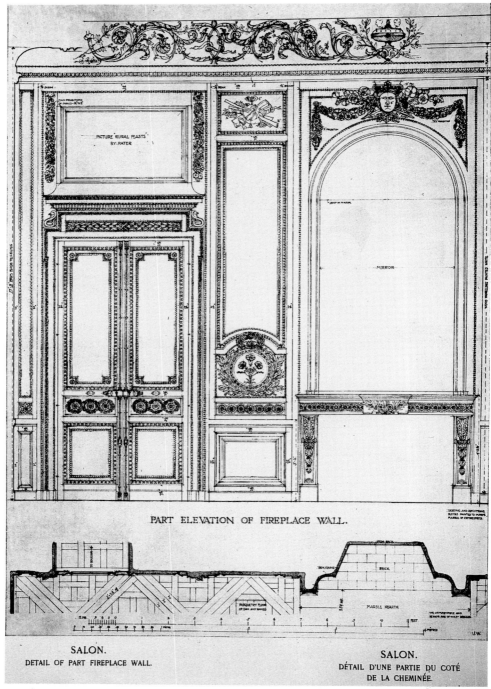

PART ELEVATION OF FIREPLACE WALL.

SALON.
DETAIL OF PART FIREPLACE WALL.

SALON.
DÉTAIL D'UNE PARTIE DU COTÉ
DE LA CHEMINÉE.

6. The Petit Trianon, vol I, plate xLi. Salon. Detail of Part Fireplace Wall.

The rich detail and embellishment of the architecture and furniture of this period, when Spain was at the height of its power and cost was apparently no object, provide a wealth of material for study. Prentice concentrated on public buildings, the most accessible, dedicating his work to Her Majesty Dona Maria Christina, the Queen Regent. The splendour to which he refers frequently is well-illustrated in the plates and elaborated upon in the texts. He identifies the materials used, for example, at the Alcala de Henares by Roderigo Gil, where the building material is stone and not marble as was generally believed (Fig. 3). The exception to the general theme of Prentice's work, for which he apologises, may be found in the plate of the Palace Morell, Palma, Majorca, later in date than most of those illustrated, and technically from outside Spain (Fig. 4). He explains the inclusion of such a rogue building for 'the elegance of its fine lines and for its stucco decoration, adorned with reliefs and coloured by an Italian artist, Antonio Soldatti'.

Although Prentice was to move on to London, he continued to work in Scotland. The Plateresque design which he submitted for the Glasgow Art Gallery competition in 1892, little known because it was unsuccessful, illustrates how well he had come to understand the style, not least through the exuberant detail shown in his perspective elevation, gathering strength in the upper wallplane and rooflines.[6]

Arnott and Wilson's *The Petit Trianon* differs from, and complements, the above works, not only in focusing on one building but also in its form. It comprises three loose leaf volumes and photographic plates. The comprehensive review of Jacques Ange Gabriel's classical masterpiece is pleasing and the Historical Note provides an enchanting backdrop.[7] The diminutive palace had been covered by several French monographs (quoted by the authors) and its importance had long been appreciated by the British, but no systematic survey had ever been carried out for publication before. John Kinross drew inspiration from the Petit Trianon for details at Manderston, Duns, and recommended it to the then younger architects as a subject for their works.[8]

The simple exterior, the authors tell, is dependent for its effect on the graceful proportions and refinement of detail, while the interior reveals ingenious spatial planning, with intimate entresol. Full attention is given to the spectacular gardens beyond. The principal staircase is elegant and stately, set in an ashlar hall to ease the transition from exterior to interior and with the exquisitely detailed wrought-iron balustrade (which evidently particularly impressed the authors) acting as centrepiece (Fig. 5). Just as the previous texts have highlighted technical and structural details of importance together with the purely aesthetic, Arnott and Wilson display a similarly all-rounded approach. They explain, for example, that the oak panelling throughout the principal rooms (originally painted bluish-green with gilding) was fastened with wooden pins, and the difficulty of framing large sections was avoided by including projecting elements, such as pilasters, to remove the need for cross rails. The skirting was painted in imitation of marble (for practical reasons) and the floors were all in oak parquetry.

The salon is of particular interest for the *avant garde* nature of the mouldings and carved work, Louis XVI in character, but Louis XV in date (Fig. 6). Here the chimneypiece of violet *breccia* is richly carved and all door and window fittings are in gilded brass.

These impressive architectural publications provide the historian with a deeper understanding of the styles under review, a greater idea of the inspiration for design afforded the architect, and rich material in the search for sources. The popularity of the volumes can be explained simply. First, they were produced at a time when eclectic design had reached its height and architects were looking abroad for inspiration more adventurously than ever before. Second, the styles illustrated lent themselves well to civic design, the leading field prior to the First World War. They are a tribute to the architects and the excellence of the subjects which they studied.

Historic Scotland,
Edinburgh

NOTES

1. For background information to this article, see D. Mays, 'Sketching Tours 1850–1914', in *Scotland and Europe 1850–1940, St Andrews Studies in the History of Architecture and Design*, 1991.

2. The full details of the publications are as follows: William James Anderson, *Architectural Studies in Italy*, Messrs Maclure Macdonald and Co: Glasgow, 1890; Andrew Noble Prentice, *Renaissance Architecture and Ornament in Spain*, B.T. Batsford: London, 1894, cover date, 1893; James Alexander Arnott and John Wilson, *The Petit Trianon*, B.T. Batsford: London, vol 1 and 2, 1907, vol 3, 1908.

3. The information cited here and below is taken from the Prefaces of the respective volumes.

4. W.J. Anderson (1863/4–1900) was trained by J. Gillespie in St Andrews from 1877, then moving to T.L. Watson of Glasgow as draughtsman, subsequently joining William Leiper. (Information courtesy of David M. Walker.)

5. A.N. Prentice (1866–1941) was born in Greenock and apprenticed to William Leiper, moving thereafter to the office of T.E. Colcutt in London. Evidence of his appreciation of the Soane Medallion Award can be found in the posthumous creation of the A.N. Prentice Bequest which gave grants to students for study in Spain: a list of the projects undertaken through this bequest is available at the RIBA, London.

6. The Prentice design for the Glasgow Art Gallery was illustrated in *The Builder*, 22 October 1892, with details and description, p. 321.

7. Arnott (d.1950) and Wilson (d.1959) were pupils of J. Russell Walker and G. Washington Browne respectively. They were never in architectural partnership as their co-operation here might suggest.

8. In the Preface, Arnott and Wilson acknowledge Kinross for his assistance.

DIDIER REPELLIN

The First Colin McWilliam Memorial Lecture: The Human Heritage: A Message from the Past Transmitted to the Future

Didier Repellin is the Architecte en Chef des Monuments Historiques, Lyon, France. This lecture was given at the Royal College of Physicians, Edinburgh, on Monday 3 December 1990. The following text is taken from a tape-recording of the lecture.

IT is a very great pleasure to be back in Edinburgh, that most civilised city. What I would like to do is to share with you tonight my experience in the field of preservation, to which Colin McWilliam devoted his whole life.

I first met Colin in Bologna in '86, at an ICOMOS meeting on training, and I was most impressed, despite the fact that we laughed all through the conference. I was impressed that he was so willing to transmit what he had learned, and to pass on his unlimited knowledge of preservation. For the first lecture I have therefore decided to talk about human heritage, because I think Colin was synonymous with human heritage. I should like to show you examples of training and sharing experience with people from other countries—in particular one experience in Singapore, and another in France with a different type of people, with prisoners.

I am starting with two cartoons by the American artist David McCaulay (Fig. 1a & b). He did these in the '70s when the fashion in the United States was to cover buildings with vinyl siding: in the cartoons we see that we can preserve the past by covering churches with plastic siding, but we also have to preserve the future by putting vinyl siding on the moon. What I like here is the link between the past and the future. That is a good thing. The bad thing is to use the wrong product just because it is in fashion.

One example is the Dome of the Rock in Jerusalem. In the '60s the beautiful lead dome was leaking and nobody knew how to repair it because the roofing and plumbing skills had been lost. There was at that time a magical new product, aluminium. So they decided to remove the lead sheets and to put on an aluminium dome. It looks absolutely awful—you just want to unscrew it! Six months ago the architect of the building visited my office. He had just noticed that the paintings underneath were peeling and the tesserae of the mosaics were falling off. The aluminium roofing had changed the hygrometry in the space between the vault and the dome itself. What they are going to do now is to remove the aluminium and put back the lead. We have to learn that new techniques have to serve buildings and not the opposite. Historic buildings are not there to be test cases for modern products.

It is the same with structural problems. At the Primatiale of St. Jean in Lyon the vault

1a and b. 'Preserving the Past' and 'Preserving the Future'. These cartoons by the American artist David McCaulay were made in the 1970s, when the fashion for covering buildings with vinyl siding was at its height in America.

over the choir fell down three times in the Middle Ages. Their insurance company at that time was not Lloyds or any such company: it was called Faith. With Faith things were much easier. I am now working on the restoration of the church. One of the two main Bureaux, the Office of Engineers, declared in a report that the spires would fall down. I simply answered, 'Thank you for the interesting news, but we've got the Holy Spirit to help us'. Fortunately we still have the spires and the towers. An old building is like an old human being. It is a little bit shaky, but it survives. And it's an old patient. You have to give old buildings the lightest possible surgery. You never need to give them lessons—instead you have to listen to them, because in return they will teach you how to do the restoration.

One important aspect is training. Colin was very interested in training, especially for architects. We should even train politicians because they think they know everything. I want to show you an example of a new training programme we have in France.

It is in a region close to Lyon, in a huge abbey called St. Antoine. It is an international organisation, because heritage now has a universal image. In France we have 175 years of experience in preservation, with not only positive results but also a lot of mistakes. We have to share our mistakes too, so that everyone can learn from them. This year we have 42 students—architects, art historians, and curators—from 21 different countries. The purpose of the course is to link theory and practice, and to let the students meet the skilled craftsmen and contractors. We therefore have a varied, two-week programme, with four workshops. The first is on stone-cutting, with a very good master-mason (Fig. 2). None of the students has ever touched any of the tools before, and it is absolutely amazing what you can get them to do. There is another workshop on stucco. The third one is on cabinet making, with the master-carpenter teaching them how to do wood panelling. The last one is mural painting, with a specialist in the field. Each day they have eight hours on the worksite, followed by a lecture in the evening. This is the fourth year of the course, and we actually enjoy it very much.

I now want to tell you about my experiences in Singapore. I spent two years in the United States between '82 and '84 on a NATO Fellowship. I went back to France to take up my present position in '85, and I thought I would never work abroad. In August '86 a fax arrived from the Singapore government: 'Your name has been given to us by the US ambassador. Could you send us a C.V.?' I sent a C.V. and they promised to be in touch. The next fax read, 'A delegation from Singapore is going to travel all over the world to study restoration and preservation. They are planning a one-day stop-over in Paris. Could you show them everything?' 'I am not working in Paris right now, but in Lyon', I replied, 'so we can split the day into two parts, with the morning in Paris and the afternoon in Lyon'.

The head of the delegation was Mrs Lee, the sister-in-law of Lee Kwan Yu, the Prime Minister, so it was easier to take decisions. All day she kept asking me, 'Why do you

2. Learning from the master mason, at one of the workshops of the international conservation course, held at the Abbaye de St. Antoine, near Lyon.

restore buildings? Is it profitable? How do you train people? How do you persuade people to do restoration?' I did not know how to answer. 'The first thing', I said, 'is to learn how to read the buildings, because historic monuments are like books. As they are very sophisticated books you have to read between the lines', 'OK', said the delegation, 'come next week and read our buildings', 'I can't come next week', I replied, but three weeks later I was in Singapore.

I bought a guide book, but I did not know anything about the history. As many of you know, Singapore is an absolutely incredible explosion of modern buildings. Three quarters of the old city has been destroyed. What is interesting is that they have four cultures. Of course, it was founded by the British in 1890 by Lord Raffles. But the Chinese house-type always has the same structure, whether it is of Chinese, Indian/Hindu or Arab/Islamic design. I also like the contrast between the modern and the old.

When I arrived they told me, 'You have three days to analyse our buildings'. On the third day they asked me to give a two-and-a-half-hour presentation about what I thought of their heritage. After two hours they began to be convinced that they had to do something to preserve the historic fabric of the city. Their reaction was very interesting. They said, 'Fine, but first we have to inform the public. Tomorrow (it was 7 pm) at 8 am we will be on TV, at 9 am on the radio, and at 11 am we'll hold a press conference'. At around noon I got a phone call from the French Embassy: 'Who are you? What are you doing here?'!

Afterwards I visited all the building sites and the training centres for craftsmen,

3. The modest house in central Singapore, chosen by the Singapore government as a test case on which to demonstrate restoration procedures in 1987.

apprentices and workers, and I noticed their unbelievable failure to transmit skills from one generation to another. I checked how many workers in Singapore knew how to re-do lime mortar or stucco. There were only three men, all over 80 years old. So the train of transmission was completely broken. How could they do restoration now? I made a list of the needs and the solutions, as well as products, services and techniques. And very quickly I realised that if I were to write a report, well, you know how it is . . . With so many reports in the world they're little read, they're just put in a drawer and that's it! So I asked if I could offer not a theoretical response but a practical one. The major buildings are almost always at least morally safe, but it is the common housing which is in very great danger. So I asked them to give me a house that we could restore together.

That's what they did. They gave me a very modest house, at a crossroads in the city centre (Fig. 3). Alongside was an empty lot, which was very useful for the worksite. I started by defining three main problem areas: the lime mortar, which had been replaced by cement, the stucco ornament, and the roof, which was made of asbestos sheeting.

First of all I went back to France and I chose seven skilled craftsmen. Six of them had never been in an aeroplane before. You can imagine how shocked they were. One day I asked one of the masons, who had never been out of his village deep in the country: 'Would you like to come with me to restore a house in Singapore?' 'Singapore', he queried, 'it's not too far?' 'No', I said, 'it's a direct flight'. But they came. (It is interesting that five of them were ill the day before we left.)

I asked the Singapore government to give me ten trainees, and they also gave me ten labourers. I had twenty-seven people, none of whom could speak each other's language. So for the first three days it was like a silent movie from the '30s. I was surprised to see that after a few hours they could understand each other, because they went to the essentials of communication: the look, the gesture, the tool and the technique. The common denominator was to restore the house.

We started with the scaffolding in April '87. It was Japanese scaffolding, which means that the height between the two landings was only about five feet. Two masons were taller than me, so they had to work on their knees! We also wanted to expose the site to public view. You know how little people usually know about a worksite—they see a black building, then one day they see scaffolding going up, a few months or years later they see it coming down again and the building is white, but in between they only see one sign: 'KEEP OUT'. We lit our worksite all night long, so that everyone who was driving by could stop and look. We invited everybody, the public, architects, contractors, just to share our experience. We were on TV every day, and in the newspapers.

The first job was the roof. They used to have V-shaped, Chinese-style tiles, but they had begun to have problems with the old tiles. Instead of analysing the cause of the problem, old tiles were simply replaced by ugly asbestos sheeting. We worked on three things: we changed the battens, using rafters which followed the shape of the tiles so that they stayed firm; we made the tiles more regular so that they fitted together better; and we made them thicker and less fragile. Actually it's much more comfortable to live under a terracotta tiled roof than under asbestos sheeting in a hot climate.

The second task was to change the mortar because of the problems with dampness caused by the use of cement mortar. We had to show them how to make traditional lime-mortar again. Finally, we had to restore the stucco decoration. One capital looked like melted ice-cream, but when we began to clean it, using a dry-cleaning method, the detail became sharp again (Fig. 4). One has to remember that there are millions of capitals in Singapore, and every one is hand-made. Behind each capital is someone who gave so much of his love, his spirit, his faith and his heart, just for this. Out of respect for the quality of human workmanship it is worthwhile transmitting traditions to the next generation.

As we only had ten days we had to work fast. At first the local trainees and workers were very lazy. We couldn't ask them to work longer than three hours. They kept stopping to drink tea or iced tea because of the heat. But by the end they were working twelve hours at a time. The important thing is to motivate workers. When you are a consultant in another country you cannot speak about style or culture because they have a different one and will not respect your point of view. All you can do is to speak of the quality of the work, and to do a very objective, scientific analysis.

Ten days later the house was finished. The last day we had a reception with the French

4. Detail of a capital on the Singapore house illustrated in Fig. 3, showing how 'melted ice cream' was transformed into crisp detail simply by cleaning the stucco.

Ambassador and all the Singapore delegation. We also had the 'French connection'—the journalists. At that time, in '87, the urban redevelopment authority in Singapore was tearing down 150 houses a day. It is interesting that, after just this one example of restoration, their ideas completely changed. Now they are stopping the demolition of old houses, and they have started a new training centre for traditional techniques. It was actually the workers themselves who were the best ambassadors. When you cannot convince the politicians you have to choose another route—you have to go through the people and the media.

The last day you can imagine what a rush it was to clean up. Five minutes before the Ambassador arrived I was still cleaning the street! I ran back to the hotel to change, and I jumped into a taxi to take me back to the crossroads. 'Are you going to the worksite?' asked the driver. 'Yes', I said, 'how did you know?' 'I saw you on TV', he replied. All the way he kept asking me, 'Why did you restore this old Chinese house? It's only an old one, a poor house. It's not worth it'. I tried to explain about the human quality of the workmanship in these old houses. When I arrived he was very surprised to see the house looking so colourful. And when I asked, 'How much do I owe you?', he answered, 'No charge for you'.

On my first visit to Singapore I brought back twenty tiles in my luggage. When the customs official opened my suitcase he said 'What is this?' 'Just a souvenir', was my reply. The next time I brought back nine kilos of mortar because I wanted to do a chemical analysis of the lime and the pigments. You can guess how easy it is to go through customs with nine kilos of white powder!

5. Slum housing in Calcutta, where even the poorest people are proud of the ingenuity and craftsmanship in their improvised shelters.

I've just come back from India. If there is a country with a human heritage, this is the one. India's problems are completely different. I was in Calcutta, which has a population of 16 million. India now has over 900 million people, with 300 millions living in slums. How can we improve these very poor houses without using the human heritage? When you see so much poverty it seems indecent to talk about the restoration of buildings. But one thing I noticed in talking to Indians is that actually they are very proud of their architecture. You can see this very subtle heritage in the way they use coconut palm leaves, mud and rice leaves, techniques which shouldn't be lost. We must not heal the body alone, but also the spirit. What is missing is the bond between the spirit and the body. Even in the slums the people are proud of their houses, and their children are laughing (Fig. 5). I was very moved. It is a mixture of desperation and hope, great hope.

The last case I want to show you is an experience with some unexpected people. One day, just after we had started cleaning the Primatiale of St Jean in Lyon, I was giving a lecture. 'Do you know?' I said, 'this is only the second time this century that we have scaffolding right up to the top of the building. This means that only one generation can see the top of the façade at close range'. When I said I should like to show this to young people—no answer. But three months later one of the supervisors came and said, 'I have some young people for you, but they are prisoners'.

'Fine', I said, although I had not expected this type of people, 'What can we do?' 'I don't know either', he replied, 'but would you like to treat this as an adventure—a nice adventure?' I agreed. He laid down three conditions. The first was that it would be impossible to keep them more than 35 minutes because they were so nervous and psychologically disturbed. There were 15 of them, between the ages of 18 and 24, all of them criminals. Secondly, it would be impossible to take them on to the scaffolding because 90 per cent of them just wanted to commit suicide. 'My goodness!' I exclaimed. And the third thing was that their IQ was very low, so I would just have to speak about very basic subjects.

The rendez-vous was in April, and I began to wonder what I could show them during a 35 minute period screwed to the ground, using only the simplest topics. All night long I was thinking about what to say to these guys who knew only the saddest things—the ugliest, the poorest, the most terrible things. In only 35 minutes, I thought, why not show them the exact opposite—the most beautiful, the most exceptional, the most demanding? I will see, 35 minutes is not long.

When they arrived I decided to keep them at ground level, of course, because that was required, and to show them the chapels. I asked the priest to take the most beautiful treasure out of the safe—the chalice. 'You are crazy', he answered, 'they will steal everything', 'Don't worry', I said, 'you will stay beside them and it will work out fine'.

I literally ran into the church, because when they arrived they were so nervous. They were yelling at each other, and they were covered in tattoos from the toes to the hair—they were absolutely incredible. There were two educators with me, so we each had to look after five of them. To catch their attention quickly I began to show them the most beautiful carvings. Of course, I didn't give them dates or style-labels—I just talked about the quality of the human work. Who did these carvings, for what purpose and how? I showed them a carved portrait of a stonemason who was a negro. 'Look', I said, 'there were many people from different cultures'. We also talked about *graffiti*: 'It isn't new', I said, 'we have *graffiti* from the 13th century'. When we arrived at the chapel where the priest was waiting he was seized by a sudden panic and sickness. But I took the pure gold chalice and told them how it was made. There was a very nice carving inside, so I turned it upside down and gave it to one of the prisoners: 'Take it and look at it'. (The priest was almost beetroot!) And he was able to inspect the chalice for himself.

Step by step we realised that they were surprised to learn that this work could be done by somebody like themselves. I told them that the craftsmen were not so well-educated; they were more often trained *in situ* on the site. Twenty, thirty five minutes later they were quite calm. I nudged one of the educators: 'There's a beautiful carving on the first landing of the scaffolding. It's not too high. If they jump down they will only break a leg'.

So I took them to the first landing and I asked one of the workers, a stone carver, to show them what he was doing. He was 19 years old, and he was carving a moulding. I showed them that every stone was different, but you cannot work in isolation, you have to work as a team, otherwise the stones won't fit together properly—it's like a society. The craftsman told them he had done the moulding three times because his first try was no good. He had worked eighteen hours in succession on the third effort. Now the

6. Cathédrale de St. Jean, Lyon, detail of a carved face near the top of the façade, dating from the 13th century. Seeing this carving was the climax of the young offenders' visit to the cathedral under restoration.

moulding was finished and he was happy. They wondered, 'How could anyone be happy after working eighteen hours in succession?' but they saw he was proud of what he had done.

Once again I jogged the educator's elbow: 'There is an exceptional carving just above'. Four hours later we were still on the scaffolding. I took them to the very top. There we found a carved face, the only face which is up there (Fig. 6). It dates from the 13th century. 'Who is it?' they asked me. 'It must be the girlfriend of one of the masons', I replied. (No priest would have come up to this height to see what they were doing.) It was interesting to see that the leaves around the head were not very well carved, but the face itself and the flowing hair were beautifully made. And we noticed some pigment: she had blue eyes and red cheeks—of course she needed a little make-up! We also showed them that cleaning one small detail like this took four days with a very soft metal tool.

The top of the scaffolding was 50 metres high, but we had to force them to go down because it was six o'clock and the works were closing. Back at the bottom they were all hanging on to the arms of the foreman, imploring him to hire them for the next morning. They wanted to start work right away.

So, I think the lesson is that quality is always something very attractive. If you motivate people there is a kind of social—I would say human—vocation to preserve the best. This is one of the main things we need to keep. Colin McWilliam had this kind of devotion, to transmit his own vocation. May I tell you, dear Christine,* that we shall keep this, the greatest souvenir of Colin, like a prisoner in the cell of our heart?

*Colin McWilliam's widow (Ed.).

Martin Millett, *The Romanization of Britain*, Cambridge University Press, 1990, Hardback, £30.

In the preface to this book Martin Millett describes his aim to write an interpretative account of the economy and society of Roman Britain based on a synthesis of modern archaeological research and publication. The book is aimed primarily at students and scholars; however, while a challenge to the specialist, it can equally be enjoyed by the general reader.

It is interesting to see some of the received ideas and opinions which have, over the years, become almost facts, well and truly debunked, but it is not necessary to have this background knowledge to appreciate the arguments, which are internally coherent.

In places the text does become over-detailed and repetitive (perhaps a result of driving points home in the lecture theatre), and his style is not always easy to digest. However, this is undoubtedly an authoritative work, and one which is based on an immense amount of research and original thought. He has gone back to basics, re-examining the evidence in the light of recent work, and writing in a manner which is sympathetic to modern scholarship; for example, referring to the 'societies' of Iron Age Britain rather than the 'natives'.

Martin Millett defines his subject as 'the interaction of Roman culture with native culture to produce the synthesis that we call Romanized'. He discusses the societies, both indigenous and from abroad, which were involved in this interaction. Sadly, this includes little consideration of those societies existing in the north where 'Romanization' was never fully developed and the Roman influence was largely military.

Throughout the book Millett develops the theme that the way Britain developed depended largely on the organisation in late pre-Roman Iron Age times. Romanization was seen to be desirable and it was a two-way acculturation process. The inherited values from the pre-Roman Iron Age were combined with Roman values to produce aspirations which were uniquely 'British' and different from the rest of the Empire. These are reflected in the art and architecture and in the pattern and type of settlement. This is also analysed at local level to show the different responses throughout Southern Britain. Again, it is a shame that the different effects of the same process in the North of Britain are not included for contrast.

In discussing the balance between the urban and rural population, Millett estimates that the urban population constituted only about 6.5% of the total, a phenomenon rarely stated, or its consequences considered. The majority of the population remained employed in agriculture and lived in houses very little different from their pre-Roman ancestors. Romanization was primarily the province of the élite, but its consequences spread to the grass-roots of society and its archaeological manifestations can eventually be seen in changing farming practice and settlement patterns throughout the countryside. 'Thus during the third quarter of the fourth century (southern) Britain was utterly Roman'.

Millett's analysis at the end of Roman Britain is again a skilful assessment of the conflicting historical and archaeological evidence and a most convincing explanation. He argues how the historical events do not necessarily coincide with an immediate economic downfall, and that society continues to function into the fifth century AD, thereby accounting for the archaeological evidence. The core of rural population remained as it had throughout the Roman administration of Britain and 'Romanization was ultimately replaced by what we might call Germanization'—but that is another study.

He concludes that Romanization should not be seen as a 'passive reflection of change but rather as an active ingredient used by people to assert, project and maintain their social status. Furthermore, Romanization should be seen as largely indigenous in its motivation, with emulation of Roman ways and styles being first a means of obtaining, or retaining, social dominance, then being used to express and define it, while its manifestations evolved'.

The book is liberally illustrated with line drawings, graphs, tables and maps which take out much of the cluttering detail from the text e.g. tables 8.1–8.5 summarise the methods by which Millett reaches his own estimate of the population of Roman Britain in the 4th century AD, leaving the text to discuss the implications of these figures. The text is thoroughly referenced to the very many authorities on which he has drawn; specialist terms are explained; Latin texts are translated.

In this book, Millett has certainly succeeded in gathering and organising the available information, as he set out to do, and he has added to this the depth of his own experience. He has bravely and skilfully set out new theories to old problems to make an exciting challenge to students and scholars. I hope that it is also a book which will be widely read and will inspire the reader to discover more about the many subjects which have been drawn together here.

Diana Murray,
National Monuments Record of Scotland

Eileen Harris, assisted by Nicholas Savage, *British Architectural Books and Writers 1556–1785*, Cambridge University Press, 1990, Hardback, £85.00.

This book is a monumental achievement in both senses of the word. Behind the project lie the inspiration and pioneering researches of two great scholars, Rudolf Wittkower and Howard Colvin. Wittkower's own explorations into British architectural books, best known through his *Palladio and English Palladianism* (1974), were left incomplete at his death. Thanks to his widow's encouragement, the material he assembled became the core of the present book. Howard Colvin's *Biographical Dictionary of British Architects* provided a model for the form of the volume, in which each writer is afforded an introductory essay, followed by a catalogue of works.

Like Colvin, Eileen Harris varies the length of each entry according to the intrinsic interest of the subject, but here this is only loosely related to an author's merit as a practising architect. Thus the entries on Halfpenny, Batty Langley and Roger Morris are all no longer than those on Gibbs or Wren. Despite his publication of Palladio's bath drawings, Lord Burlington is not even given a cross reference, while one of Britain's most distinguished writer-architects, Sir John Vanbrugh, is justifiably excluded because his plays had no direct architectural relevance.

The important consequence of decisions such as these is that the focus of study of British architectural history is shifted sideways. At a time when travel was slow and tedious, it was easier to buy or borrow a book than to tour new buildings. Thus the less 'orthodox' views of writers such as Ralph and Langley must have reached a larger audience, and appealed to a wider social range, than what we now consider to be mainstream (i.e. aristocratic) architectural taste. These prolific and influential writers can now shed their maverick connotations and be reinstated in the centre of the architectural stage.

Harris and Savage must have had difficulty in limiting this open-ended subject. They have omitted country house guides, books on gardens (unless a writer also wrote on architecture) and foreign books (unless published in Britain). On the other hand, books on bridge-building and on practical subjects such as the problems of smoking chimneys have been included. It is delightful to learn of Carmichael's *The Edinburgh Smoke Doctor* (1757), dedicated to none other than Lord Provost George Drummond.

The analysis of architectural writings involves a complex interplay of ideas. First of all, the books discussed are likely to be rare and, if illustrated, works of art in themselves. Secondly the circumstances of publication must be investigated, the sources of ideas examined and the influence assessed. The writers of this volume have taken up this challenge with an enviable, easy confidence. It would be ungracious to quibble with details. One can only applaud this scholarly achievement, which will remain an essential and most readable reference work for many generations.

Deborah Howard, University of Edinburgh

The Architecture of the Scottish Renaissance, RIAS Edinburgh International Festival Exhibition, 1990

Among the delights of last year's Edinburgh Festival and one of the distinguished contributions of the RIAS to its 150th anniversary was the exhibition *The Architecture of the Scottish Renaissance* held in the Incorporation's rooms in Rutland Square. To go with the exhibition the organisers—led by Charles McKean—produced an illustrated catalogue. Edited by Deborah Howard, the catalogue (good value at £4 per copy still available from the RIAS Bookshop) gives an excellent overview of the subject. In eleven short sections contributors explain the essential background of King and Court, Parliament, The Burgh, Town Houses, Interiors, Gardens, The Profession of Architect, and two special short chapters on Heriot's Hospital and the Country House.

This last is a characteristically refreshing and polemical account by Charles McKean which clearly draws our attention to the truly advanced nature of these houses. The term *corps de logis* stretches matters rather for this reviewer but it is abundantly plain that Craigievar, for example, is made up of a series of *appartements*, that is, a self contained principal chamber, with a secondary and support rooms *en suite*—an idea only recently perfected at Chambord. The essential difference is that we stacked them one on top of the other, and finished the whole off, again Chambord fashion, with an agreeable display of fine architectural 'follies' on the roof. They are no more castles—in the rude and defensive sense—than are their north Italian and English contemporaries—e.g. Bolsover Castle, c. 1610.

Amazingly this exhibition and catalogue are the first treatment of Renaissance architecture in Scotland since MacGibbon and Ross, and their volumes (whose centennial comes next year) can hardly be said to count. In any other place in Europe it would be unbelievable that such a significant group of buildings and the culture which produced them should be ignored, or worse still, denigrated; it would be a sick joke anywhere but in Scotland. Why this should be so is a very complex issue, and it will need to be unravelled and explained by Dr Howard and her colleagues before the true story can be told. Whereas English history is seen as national history (indeed, since the turn of the 18th and 19th centuries, international as it is shared first by the USA, then others), Scottish history is perceived as just that, and no more. Seen from a unionist perspective this makes some sense. Hume, to a degree, then certainly Scott and Macaulay demeaned Scottish affairs in favour of the stronger, more promising good of Great Britain. Scottish culture is made romantic and darkly attractive, but marginalised. This is manifestly unfair, and it has made for poor history.

Self-denigration can be mistaken for that most excellent Scottish trait, scepticism. The very foundation of Scottish intellectual activity, scepticism becomes destructive when applied to our architecture of the 16th century. Why, for example, if the residents of the Highlands do not deserve a reputation as barbaric savages, introduce A.S. Piccolomini's conventional account of a pilgrimage in the 'wilderness' (1435), or Sir Anthony Weldon's equally conventional, and literary, 'Judas had sooner find the grace of repentance, than a tree to hang himself on' (1560s), when the highly coloured vision of James II's glittering Renaissance court—as depicted at Siena Cathedral—is passed over without comment?

It is partly because these are among the very few accounts we have, and we have been taught to rely on contemporary comment and upon documentation to write scientific architectural history. These are doubtless colourful as well as rare accounts but surely a Pope seeking to establish the rigours of his early service to Church, or an English courtier visiting in the murky political climate of the mid 16th century will arouse scepticism? Yes, of course, but sadly not enough.

An effect of this is to undervalue or misread the monument because it is not backed up by 'requisite' documentation. Stirling comes off badly in this respect: the King's Knot is clearly an extraordinary creation—massive formal garden platforms made of sloped earth—which we might confidently expect to be a work of James VI, and thus late 16th century. But since the royal household accounts do not exist for that period—they were lost at sea between here and Denmark—a diligent search for other entries is made, and, as there is a reference to small garden works c. 1623 the King's Knot is assigned to that period. However a painting of the late 17th century does not show the King's Knot: therefore it is assumed that it must be later still! A healthier scepticism about evidence is needed here.

Renaissance, as a term, is a bit like a piece of string—it can be as long as you like. It used to stretch all the way to 1840, but that absurdity is now given up in most places. I wonder if anything after Della Porta can be Renaissance in any real sense. But Dr Howard extends it to 1660 or thereabouts, and is characteristically persuasive when stressing its Europe-wide nature, not always dependent on Tuscany. That very interesting argument will doubtless be expanded on in her forthcoming fuller book and we await that with anticipation.

The major monument of that later period is Heriot's Hospital in Edinburgh, designed as early as 1627. This great quadrangular building, in full sight from crowded Edinburgh on open ground surrounded by fine gardens and orchards, may have derived from a variety of sources—from Serlio's Ancy-le-Franc at Fontainebleau, perhaps with a hint from contemporary Salomon de Brosse in the square domes, or even Palladio in the rhythm of fenestration. It was the gift of the goldsmith of James VI and Queen Anne and 'represents a climax in Scottish Renaissance architecture. It stands alone as a privileged piece . . .' (p 15). It does seem extraordinary—almost a Scottish prodigy building—if it is viewed from the perspective of Edinburgh. But it does not seem so strange if we see it in the context of British court life. We all know that James and Anne had moved to England and that they had fulfilled the promise of Stirling of the 1590s quite spectacularly. Why is this not allowed to be part of an account of the Scottish Renaissance? Presumably it is because it belongs to England. Even though it was James and Anne who alone employed Jones, first as artistic advisor and 'masque maker' and then for the Banqueting House in Whitehall, and the Queen's House at Greenwich—both of pan-European stature; and even though James and Anne secured Salomon and Isaac de Caus to teach architecture and other related subjects to Prince Henry and Prince Charles—an association which culminated in Wilton House and Garden. Never mind Charles' picture collection—the pride of the Prado—nor the family's patronage of Van Dyck to decorate their buildings.

If I appear to grumble a bit about definitions and methodology I would not wish any reader to assume that *The Architecture of the Scottish Renaissance* is anything less than first rate, and you all ought to not only possess a copy of the catalogue but should read it—alas the exhibition with its excellent models is now disbanded, but most of it has been remounted at Stirling Castle. Some of the issues it raises require very serious thought— not only about the Renaissance period, but about Scottish culture more generally—we sit complaining about the rain when there are unrecognised Michaelangelos in the loft!

William Brogden
Scott Sutherland School of Architecture, Aberdeen.